RICHARD OWEN

Scotland 1810   *Indiana 1890*

RICHARD OWEN

*Distinguished member of an illustrious family, captain in the
Mexican War, colonel in the War Between the States,
eminent professor in Indiana University, contributor
to the sciences of geology, meteorology, and seis-
mology, first president of Purdue University,*

1872-1874

RICHARD OWEN

Scotland 1810   *Indiana 1890*

By

Victor Lincoln Albjerg

Professor of History

THE ARCHIVES OF PURDUE

NUMBER 2   MARCH 1946

Paperback ISBN: 978-1-55753-962-5
Epub ISBN: 978-1-55753-958-8
Epdf ISBN: 978-1-55753-957-1

This book was brought back into circulation thanks to the generous support of Purdue University's Sesquicentennial Committee.

CONTENTS

ILLUSTRATIONS

Chapter I

BACKGROUNDS AND BEGINNINGS

ROBERT OWEN, father of Richard Owen, was born in the eighteenth century, yet spiritually he belonged to the twentieth. Though reared in the era of the ancient regime, he championed equality; though a contemporary of Adam Smith, he advocated the doctrines later proclaimed by Karl Marx; though he was taught the tenets of fundamentalism, he endorsed the principles embodied in the *Origin of Species;* and though he lived in the heyday of Malthusianism, he relieved his employees of fear and want one hundred and fifty years before the announcement of the Atlantic Charter. He practiced big-business principles before Henry Ford's father inoculated his son with the ideas of free enterprise. In the theory of education he anticipated Froebel; in criminology, Lombroso. He was the embodiment of the visionary and the realist, the humanitarian and the efficiency expert, the talker and the doer, "the terrible bore and the salt of the earth." In his time he was ridiculed and admired, feared and loved, lionized and shunned. Though he was puzzling to his contemporaries, he was an unusually able man sensitive to the inhuman exploitation of the working class whose lot he strove to ease—an employer in the role of a labor leader.

Robert Owen was born in 1771 in Newtown, central Wales. His father was the local postmaster as well as a saddler and ironmonger. Robert was a precocious lad who displayed such intellectual promise that he was made assistant to the master almost as soon as he entered the village school. At ten, his formal education ceased and his initiation into business commenced. By the time he was twenty, he was the successful foreman of a Manchester textile mill that employed 500 millhands. Of such superior quality was the commodity of his production that its reputation extended to Glasgow and commanded a price considerably above that of other textiles.

Owen was in even greater demand than his product, and consequently in succession he managed several mills. This enterprising young man, in conjunction with several others, purchased the cotton mill owned by David Dale of New Lanark, Scotland. Thus, by the time he was twenty-eight he was the managing partner of the largest and best mill above the Tweed, and apparently on the road to huge profits and enormous wealth. Soon thereafter he fell in love with Anne Caroline, the oldest daughter of Dale, and on September 30, 1799, he married her. On her mother's side she could trace her ancestry to noble blood. She was the great-granddaughter of the Earl of Breadalbane's third son, Colin Campbell, who was repudiated by his family for marrying a farmer's daughter. When Anne Caroline was twelve years of age her mother died, and thenceforth until her marriage she was in charge of her father's household and her four younger sisters. Though her formal education stopped in early adolescence, her intellectual development continued under the stimulation of visiting Presbyterian ministers and professors of religion who frequented the Dale home.

But gold and greed had less appeal to Owen than humble humanity. He believed that mankind was essentially good. Only institutions, he said, perverted man. He spent his whole career reiterating the principle that people are made what they are by circumstances over which they have no control. He insisted that "man becomes a wild and ferocious savage, a cannibal, or a highly civilized being, according to the circumstances in which he may be placed by birth." He would not hold the barbarian accountable for his savagery, the man-eater for his cannibalism, or the Scotch murderer for his brutality. As an environmental-ist, he held that man was a creature of his circumstances, that society could mold its own character with mathematical preci-sion, and that men could be made universally good and happy. According to him, human nature was one of the most change-able things in the world. He held the views later expressed by Thomas Henry Huxley: "The intelligence which has con-verted the brother of the wolf into the guardian of the flock ought to be able to do something toward curbing the instincts of savagery in civilized man."

To curb man's exploitation of man, he exhausted his energy and sacrificed his fortune. He upbraided his fellow-manufactur-ers for their sensitiveness toward their dead machinery, and their callousness toward their living operatives. He berated Southern slavocracy for holding in subjection millions of Negroes; he rebuked English millocracy for condemning hundreds of thous-ands of children to servitude. Fourteen hours a day was the customary schedule for children nine years of age. Conscience-less employers worked children of six twelve hours a day.

To keep children from evil, and to keep the machines run-ning, they chained the youngsters to their machines. Roused before daybreak, they toiled until after sunset. Put to bed with supper in their hands, next morning they were awakened clutching the unfinished and unappetizing meal, and were car-ried or driven to the mill to resume the unending rush.

This was the environment which Owen, the environmentalist, insisted demoralized the victims of the new industrialism. Upon his acquisition of the mill, New Lanark was little better than the average factory town. The mills employed 2,000 laborers, of whom 500 were children apprenticed from the parish work-house. Owen described them as a "a collection of the most igno-rant and destitute from all parts of Scotland, possessing the usual attributes of poverty and ignorance. They were generally indolent and much addicted to theft, drunkenness and falsehood."

[7]

Owen, the environmentalist, would alter the surroundings and thereby transform the personnel. New Lanark was reorganized largely on a co-operative rather than a competitive basis. He paid maximum salaries instead of distributing bloated dividends. He shortened hours and placed emphasis upon comfort, security, and character, and not upon earnings, surplus, and capital investment. And, paradoxically, the firm prospered. The object of life was made the romance of living rather than the quest for wealth. Such improvements were effected that New Lanark won so enviable a reputation that it was visited by social reformers, statesmen, and royalty from all Europe. Owen envisaged the application of his system to Scotland, then to England, and finally to all the world.

He conceived "wealth made abundant beyond the wants and wishes of the human race," and its accumulation as a basis for the inauguration of universal socialism. "The grand question now to be solved," he said in 1818, "is not how a sufficiency of wealth may be produced, but how the excess of riches, which may most easily be created, may be generally distributed throughout society advantageously for all, and without prematurely disturbing the existing institutions or arrangements of any country." Man has not the wit, he would observe, to distribute what science has enabled him so embarrassingly to produce. As a precursor of the consumption school, not yet founded, "Owen the visionary" had a practical solution: increase the consuming power of the masses by raising their wages. He was accused of being ahead of his time; perhaps his contemporaries were a century and half behind schedule.

Important as was his co-operative experiment at New Lanark in an age of orthodox capitalism, Owen's soundest claim to fame is his establishment of kindergarten schools, the first of their kind in Great Britain. Theretofore, children in school had been viewed as sprouts of the devil, potential criminals, the basis of whose training should be restriction. Owen realized

[8]

that a ship could not be steered unless it was in motion, and similarly, that personal development was impossible with a stagnant and inhibited mentality. Studying, he said, could not be induced by wrath or the rod, but by invoking the pupil's interest. He had no patience with either rewards or punish- ments. The pupils were taught to find the best incentive in the pleasure of learning, and in the spirit of innocent emulation that springs up naturally when children are learning in groups. Schooling ought to be like play, that is, interesting. Dances, games, and story-telling formed a large part of the day's work for little pupils whose ages ran as low as two. Both the content of the curriculum and the ages of the pupils were more uncon- ventional than would be Russian institutions grafted upon the home town of Calvin Coolidge.

Owen urged that classical education should not be thrust down the throats of all its unwilling victims. He added utili- tarian courses to his curriculum instead of the academic froth, which constituted too large a portion of the intellectual diet in schools. He advocated free, universal education a hundred years before it became a reality. Owen's mistake was in appear- ing on the scene in the era of George III instead of in that of Lloyd George.

Yet he was not altogether unappreciated. Lords and bishops reflected upon his methods with a meritorious sympathy. The Duke of Kent, father of Queen Victoria, associated with him on intimate terms. Nicholas of Russia, the future Tsar, made a trip to New Lanark, and hoped to place Owen at the head of a colony in Russia. When Owen traveled upon the conti- nent, he was warmly received by Cuvier, La Place, and Madame de Staël; while in Geneva he met Oberlin, Fellenberg, and Pestalozzi; while in Germany he discussed his prospective reforms with Alexander von Humboldt.

While individual philosophers might glow with enthusiasm and a distant Tsar might meditate upon the merits of a co-operative society, the rulers of England, confronted with real situations, had to be practical, a fact, which, according to Disraeli, required them to repeat the blunders of their predecessors. The Tory Jew believed that the duty of statesmen was "to effect those changes by legislation which if neglected would be accomplished by revolution"; while Macaulay advised Owen's contemporaries to "reform, if you would preserve."

In 1600 Bruno was burned at the stake for teaching that the earth was not the center of the universe. Newton was pronounced "impious and heretical" by a large school of philosophers for declaring that the force which holds the planets in their orbits was universal gravitation. By the English upper-classes Owen was thought to be as unreliable as Bruno and Newton were at one time supposed to be. He and his ideas were ignored until they became disturbing. To England's reactionary government under Lord Liverpool, Owen's co-operation seemed even newer than the New Deal to American Bourbons. The English government after the wars of the French Revolution, therefore, merely pursued demobilization instead of reconstruction. Lord Sidmouth's prescription for unemployment was the Manchester Massacre in 1819. Consequently, a less obtuse man than Owen might have sensed that England was not then altogether hospitable to a co-operative movement.

But he was by no means deterred. He was endlessly hopeful and sure of success. To him the millenium seemed always just around the proverbial corner, and at one time that corner was a bend in the Wabash. New America, less influenced by social and economic inhibitions than old England, was chosen as the scene of the new venture. In 1825 Owen bought New Harmony from the Rappites, who sold it for $150,000. It comprised about 30,000 acres, some of which were improved. Here were fine orchards, and an extensive vineyard embracing eighteen acres. The village was composed of thirty-five brick, forty-five frame, and about one hundred log houses. The most imposing edifice was the town hall, a huge cruciform structure measuring 145 feet in length with arms 27 feet in width. More appreciated by Owen were the factories with their machinery intact.

To this outpost of co-operation came some 800 heterogeneous people. Among them were earnest devotees of Owen's co-operative faith, others who were attracted by the somewhat unconventional nature of the enterprise, and human hyenas who stalked the experiment until, in its wobbly stage, they pounced upon it to satisfy their own money lust. Owen exercised no discrimination in the admission of members to his community, his faith in environment being so unshakeable that he believed New Harmony would mold its people to its purposes.

In two addresses in the House of Representatives, with senators, representatives, supreme court judges, the diplomatic corps, and the President in attendance, on February 25 and March 7, 1825, Owen outlined what he hoped to do on the banks of the Wabash. Soon thereafter he arrived in New Harmony, where he remained less than a month to arrange the details of organizing his community, leaving their execution to deputies. On July 17 he returned to England and saw no more of his enterprise until January of the following year. Simultaneously with his return an aggregation of distinguished scholars, known as the "Boatload of Knowledge," arrived in New Harmony. Among them were Thomas Say, American zoologist, C. A. Le Sueur, a French naturalist, Dr. Gerard Troost, afterwards state geologist of Tennessee, Madame Fretageot, a French woman of unusual ability who assumed responsibility for the education of the girls, Miss Lucy Sistaire, who later married Thomas Say, and Joseph Neef, who had been a coadjutor of Pestalozzi and later became the director of a boys' school. He had conducted upon Pestalozzian principles at Schuylkill Falls such an institution, in which Admiral Farragut had been a student. This nucleus of intellectual aristocrats drew other learned men to

[11]

the Hoosier Mecca of learning until the meetings of the Phila-
delphia Academy of Science resembled a Purdue history class
when the Boilermaker team plays Indiana at Bloomington.

While science flourished, economics languished and the community's name belied its discord. Though seven constitutions
were drafted for the colony in two years, happiness and prosperity remained elusive. Owen's equal pay for different types
of service created dissent; and before long some of the disappointed nonequalitarians broke away from the mother community and established a settlement of their own, divided further
by mutual contempt than by distance. Eventually there were
ten distinct communities, whose drudges toiled while the drones
crowded around for the loaves and fishes. Owen's followers
were torn by too many cleavages, religious, economic, and phil-
osophic. By the middle of 1828 the New Harmony community
project had failed utterly at a cost of more than $200,000 to
Owen.

A dissolution of the project ensued. Soon after the formation
of the community, Owen had sold half of the land to William
Maclure; the rest he had never assigned to the community.
So most of this he conveyed to his sons, who paid him an
annuity of $1500. New Harmony thereafter became another
Indiana village, and yet not just another Hoosier community,
for many of the finest spirits who had come there to join the
Owen experiment remained to illumine its distinctive future.

Though Owen bade farewell to that Harmony which had
proved so discordant, he still hoped to exhibit to the struggling
and dissatisfied world a community of concord where justice,
equality, fraternity, and happiness would prevail. He envisioned
local contentment and prosperity extended to national bound-
aries, and, finally, projected to every corner of the world. He
would yet become the social Luther Burbank. Financially
depleted but overflowing with hope, he went to Mexico, where
he exhausted considerable time and energy in promoting a

community. He negotiated with the Mexican minister to London for the entire province of Coahuila and Texas. In October, 1828, he arrived in Vera Cruz and thence journeyed to Mexico City, where he had an audience with Santa Anna and was promised a strip of land 150 miles wide which would extend from sea to sea. Owen insisted upon religious freedom within this region, whereupon the Mexican Congress vetoed the venture. Later he returned to England and attempted to estab- lish three other co-operative areas, one each in England, Scotland and Wales; but these merely repeated the failures in America.

Owen still carried on, but by 1830 he had lost the confidence of the propertied classes. What was even more damaging to his cause was his alienation of religiously minded people. Even when he was a youth, the conflicting claims of the various creeds had aroused doubts in his mind as to the authenticity of the respective doctrines. Instead of subscribing to any one of these, he formulated a faith in a universal spirit that embodied the tenets of deism. In turn he extended his charity and humani- tarianism to all the world, irrespective of creed, color, or race; and thus he became a pioneer in the modern ethical movement.

On his return from Mexico in the spring of 1829, he went directly to Cincinnati, where he had arranged the year before to meet any American clergyman in debate on religion. The Rev- erend Alexander Campbell of Bethany, West Virginia, leader of the Disciples of Christ, had been chosen to defend the assaults of the infidel. They met in a Methodist Church and, in a religious marathon lasting eight days, the contenders spoke alternately for an hour each before an audience whose interest never flagged. Owen argued his contention that all religions were founded upon ignorance and, therefore, were the source of evil and the foe of progress. After such a blast at organized religion, church leaders published distorted accounts of his socialistic theories and exaggerated his rationalistic views on marriage. Owen the visionary, they said, was dangerous.

Since he could no longer expect any following from the middle and upper classes for his co-operative projects, he turned for popular support to the laboring element. Consequently, he organized the Grand Consolidated Labor Union in 1833. Since it challenged more threateningly the propertied class than had any other of his actions, it called forth more drastic response. Lock-outs and savage repressive measures were instituted against laborers, and within a year the Grand Consolidated Union collapsed. Owen's career had passed its peak of usefulness. Yet he continued for twenty years to work tirelessly and to give of his substance for the establishment of Equitable Labor Exchanges and to sponsor co-operative distribution. Even when "his body was turning cold," he was still projecting plans for reforming society.

Though Owen's ideas were not accepted in his day, the practical Scandinavians have put into operation on a national scale many of his co-operative proposals. Russia has gone even further than he advocated. A man sprung from poverty to substantial wealth by the time that he was forty, who willingly placed his fortune at the service of his fellowmen, was more than just a dreaming visionary. He had glimpsed what complacent and remorseless noblemen refused to see—the pitiless exploitation of human resources—and he had endeavored to devise an economic amelioration. But entrenched arrogance and selfishness defended the status quo by mumbling "God's will immutable."

Owen was perhaps of greater influence in America than he had been in England. He has been credited with being responsible for the establishment of the following "firsts" in this country: the first kindergarten; the first free school; the first coeducational school; the first industrial school; the first prohibition of liquor by administrative decree.

The radical humanitarian who was responsible for this was the father of Richard Owen, first president of Purdue University. Though Richard's mother was not so spectacular as was his father, she was nevertheless a woman of high idealism, unusual charm, and great devotion. She yielded readily to her husband's humanitarian proposals and would, except for failing health, have followed him to New Harmony. She died in 1831 in Scotland.

This was the admirable and fortunate heritage of Richard Owen. Yet his father invariably maintained that a son could no more inherit his father's wooden head than he could inherit his father's wooden leg. He insisted that environment was the sole determinant of an individual's development. Fortunately he was unable to prevent the operation of the principles of genetics even before they were discovered, and he took seriously the problem of providing his children with felicitous surround-ings. Furthermore, Robert Owen notwithstanding, some of the splinters of the father embedded themselves in the son.

Chapter II

YEARS OF PREPARATION

ICHARD, the youngest of eight children, was born in 1810. He had four brothers and three sisters. His oldest brother died in infancy, Anne in 1831, and Mary in 1832. The surviving children were Robert Dale, born in 1801, William in 1802, Jane Dale in 1805, David Dale in 1807.

The Owen home was a refuge of culture and happiness, and Richard's early years were distinctly cheerful and wholesome. His father, a devotee of Pestalozzian principles, allowed wide latitude in the rearing of his children, none of whom was ever subjected to a mental or an emotional strait-jacket. Parental guidance there was, but no dictation; and the children grew as normally and as freely as nature itself. There were bantering and hilarity but never unrestrained boisterousness, and the youngsters developed with the dignity and maturity that come with the exercise of personal responsibility.

Since the births of the children were separated by only a year or two, they constituted a family group with a community of interest. Their education was carefully directed and supervised by their conscientious parents, for Owen outlined the general nature of the program and left its execution to his wife while he went about on his promotional activity and speaking tours. She gave special emphasis to their religious training; and Owen, in spite of his devotion to deism, raised no objection to the Presbyterian inculcation.

Braxfield, the Owen home on the Clyde at New Lanark, was a beautiful structure situated on an attractive site. The forty-acre estate that surrounded the house was forested with majestic trees and a dense underbrush threaded with paths and broken with playgrounds. The clear waters of the Clyde provided swimming holes where Richard and his brothers and sisters splashed in summers; in the fall there were nutting parties in the woods, and in rainy weather or during the winter months the children transferred their activity into the house, where not even their father's study escaped utilization in the quest for pleasure.

Richard, like his older brothers and sisters, received his early education under a private tutor, but later entered New Lanark's manual training and grammar schools, which had been founded by his father. From there he entered the educational institute of Emmanuel Fellenberg at Hofwyl, in Switzerland. His father, on a European tour in 1818, had selected it for the education of his sons in preference to the establishments of Pestalozzi or Oberlin. It was operated on Pestalozzian principles, and there Richard spent most of his time on natural sciences. Of these, he specialized in chemistry. He also took instruction in gymnastics and military drill, as well as in French and German, which accomplishments he utilized in later life. After spending three years there he returned to Scotland and continued his education at the Andersonian Institution of Glasgow, where he pursued courses in chemistry and physics under the instruction of Dr. Andrew Ure.

In January, 1828, Richard in company with his father and two of his brothers, Robert Dale and David Dale, arrived in New Harmony. For a short period after their arrival Richard engaged in teaching. During vacation periods his keen interest in geology and nature's great outdoors impelled him to join his brothers on long horseback rides over the surrounding territory. In time Madame Marie Fretageot, active and energetic manager of Maclure's affairs, reminded the Owen brothers of their lack of diligence and invited them to co-operate in her

[17]

printing enterprise. But in their youthful self-assurance they scorned such advice and averred that they had greater prospects in mind.

Whether Richard was stung by the needling words of Madame Fretageot or driven by his own ambition, he soon abandoned the teaching and equestrian pursuits. For a short while he tried farming in Lancaster County, Pennsylvania. Not finding that to his satisfaction, he floated down the Ohio to Cincinnati and for three years worked in a brewery under the direction of his friend Dr. William Price. But like other Owens he was drawn back to New Harmony, where he had acquired some land of his own, which he operated for seven years until the outbreak of the Mexican War.

Richard Owen approached farming from the viewpoint of a scientist. He fertilized his fields, stocked his pastures, and equipped his farm with implements he could buy or make, and marketed his surplus in the highest market. When one of his hired men had packed some meat in a careless fashion that resulted in its putrefaction, Owen upbraided him as a "great rascal." But he found it difficult to evict tenants from one of his houses long after they had become delinquent in their rent.

His homestead was lacking in one essential: there was no helpmate. His sister Jane Dale had married Robert Fauntleroy; David Dale had committed himself to Caroline Neef, William to Mary Bolton, all of New Harmony. Richard was left in loneliness, and this isolation filled him with a terrible sense of detachment. To escape this fate he accompanied David Dale to the Neef home and thereby implemented the law of supply and demand in the field of affection. Very soon he demanded, or perhaps requested, the hand of Anne Eliza Neef, sister of Caroline.[1] Anne was only seventeen, and just before they were married her mother cautioned the prospective husband, "Remem-

---

[1] Richard's previous marriage, in 1828, had been terminated by the death of his wife.

ber, Richard, that she is my baby. Indeed, she is only a child. If I let you marry her, you must treat her as she is—a child." "Yes," said Richard, and that pledge he never violated through their fifty years of married life.

On March 23, 1837, in a famous triple wedding, William married Mary Bolton, David Dale married Caroline Neef, and Richard married Anne Eliza Neef. According to Robert Dale Owen, Richard's bride was "the loveliest and prettiest." Furthermore, she could sing, dance, and play the piano well. Robert Dale insisted that she "would be admired for her ladylike appearance even in fashionable society." The wedding ceremony was solemnized in the Neef home. Since the trousseaus of the brides had not arrived on the date set for the wedding, the young brides were attired for the occasion in calico gowns. In the afternoon the wedding party went for a long horseback ride, and in the evening there was a wedding ball to which all residents of New Harmony and half of those living in Posey County were invited. On the following day all the newlyweds hired a carriage and drove to Mammoth Cave, where Richard compelled Cupid to share affections with stalagmites and stalactites. Upon their return to New Harmony all of them, at the request of Robert Owen, took up residence in the big Owen mansion where Robert Dale and Jane Dale were already living with their families. It is a tribute to their character and mutual toleration that they lived in congenial relationship for three years, and that there was no secession until additional Owens arrived to necessitate separate establishments.

Richard's father-in-law had been a soldier under Napoleon, and after the cessation of the revolutionary disturbances he had taken up educational work. Though he had changed pursuits, he had retained a blunt and offhand style of speech, reinforced with occasional army profanity, an accomplishment that was no asset to him as a professor. But he also had educational ideas that were as revolutionary as the political doctrines he had championed with his musket. As coadjutor of Pestalozzi at Iverdun, Switzerland, he had acquired a European reputation, and through the influence of William Maclure he had been brought in the Boatload of Knowledge to New Harmony.

Joseph Neef proclaimed that, in his humble opinion, "education is nothing but the gradual unfolding of the faculties and powers which Providence chooses to bestow on the noblest work of his sublime creation, man." Education was not knowledge but the unfolding of childish powers. The aim of education, therefore, should be expression and not repression. He was proficient in several modern languages, an accomplished musician and an engaging conversationalist. In his home was an atmosphere of culture that would have attracted Richard had there been no other motive for going there. Whatever intellectual interests Richard possessed, and they were obviously many, were whetted by his association with his father-in-law.

Absorbing as were farming and teaching, Richard forsook both upon the outbreak of the Mexican War in 1847. His distinguished brother, Robert Dale, was then a member of Congress; and through his influence Richard was commissioned in April, 1847, a captain of the 16th United States Infantry regiment under General Taylor. His headquarters were at Monterey most of the time, and he was charged with the management of the provision trains, a duty he executed with fidelity. During intervals between the succession of duties, Richard found time to study Spanish. He was favorably impressed not only with the country's language, but also with the country. He wrote his wife, "It is decidedly the finest climate I ever lived in and were it annexed and inhabited by Americans I should try hard to persuade you and some other friends to settle here. There is scarcely any sickness here . . . ." In August, 1848, he returned to civilian life.

Upon his return from Mexico he joined his brother, David Dale, who was in the midst of preparations for a survey of the

Northwest territory. Richard spent the fall and winter equip-
ping himself for his new duties, and during the summer of
1848 the expedition mapped the region along the southern shores
of Lake Superior and in northern Minnesota as far as Lake of
the Woods. His duties consisted chiefly of recording the
barometric pressures of the region and the making of illustrative
sketches and diagrams. Most of the woodcuts in his brother's
report were the work of Richard, and the success of the expedition was in no small degree owing to his skill and dependability.

Teaching, however, was more attractive to him than was
surveying. Consequently he accepted when Colonel Thornton
Johnson, who at Drennen Springs, Kentucky, had organized the
"Western Military Institute," offered him a chair in the natural
sciences. The natural science chair was elongated into a davenport, for he soon found himself teaching not only the sciences
but also French, German, Spanish, military science, and fencing.
As Owen lectured in the different fields, he figuratively slid
along the davenport, halting over the proper designation, holding forth for an hour, and then moving to the next cushion to
pontificate in an entirely different course. He carried on in
this multiple capacity for nine years, during the last three of
which he took courses in medicine at the Medical College of
Nashville. The Western Military Institute, of which Richard
Owen had become part owner, had been moved to Nashville,
where it had become an affiliate of Nashville University. In
1858 the degree of Doctor of Medicine was conferred upon him.
During his leisure time he amused himself in painting and
drawing, in both of which he acquired considerable proficiency.
He still found sufficient time to write a *Key to the Geology of
the Globe*, of which a reviewer in the *North American Review*
of July 18, 1857, said, "Unity of plan and uniformity of
courses are the germinal idea of his system." A copy was sent
to Alexander von Humboldt, which he appreciatively acknow-
ledged and many of the generalizations of which he accepted.

With the students Dr. Owen was popular, as was emphatically attested during the War Between the States; and if slavery and secession had not divided the nation, he might well have become one of the leading educators of the South. But his outlook was out of harmony with that section's beliefs. In the heart of the Cotton Kingdom he condemned the stratification of the population into master and slave. With fervor he proclaimed that "here amid nature's wild, human hope expanded, a new regime was founded, and America took up her appointed mission of exemplifying to the world the inalienable rights of man." This descendant of an equalitarian father decried the stratification of society on the basis of wealth or caste. To southern gentlemen and their ladies he announced, "Talk not of aristocracy of family or of wealth in this free country. Honest and honorable parentage is certainly a recommendation . . but to attempt to build upon it any personal superiority or immunity is contemptible and the reliance of only shallow minds." For Andrew Johnson, once apprenticed tailor, and then rising statesman, he had a high regard. Southern aristocracy might frown upon this representative of the poor whites, but Owen declared that this promising young man, though he had a humble beginning, exemplified Burke's maxim that there was "no excellence without great labor." Should Johnson attain higher office, Owen would not hold it against the aspiring young man that he had at one time been a laborer.

Owen believed that the claims of mechanical labor equalled in respectability those of any other pursuit. He deplored that laborers and inventors were "proscribed in social intercourse, trammeled in their spheres of usefulness and their noble pride as men, and the most hallowed feelings as husband, parent, and brother outraged by the iniquitous prejudice that stamps degradation and inferiority upon holy, honorable and manly occupation." The South, he said, paid homage to Clay, Calhoun, and Jackson, but to Eli Whitney, they owed a mausoleum.

[22]

With his high regard for labor, he held in high esteem the toiler, regardless of his color. For the white man who worked in productive effort he sensed a social kinship, a unity of purpose in the creative enterprise that would enrich and ennoble citizenship. With the colored man who cultivated corn and cotton he shared his pride of achievement and his satisfaction in contribution. Though he respected the Negro toiler, he detested the system of bondage which enslaved the colored people to their masters. To Owen slavery was a negation of justice, an insult to humanity, and a blight that debased the master and degraded the slave.

Until the opening of the War Between the States, he was a Democrat. The firing on Fort Sumter made him a Union Democrat. In the heat of the Dred Scott decision he called upon the South, and no less the North, for tolerance: "If . . . there are great and agitating questions, regarding which we cannot take the same views, let us give each other credit for good intentions, and listen, if possible, dispassionately to all arguments on either side, provided these arguments are advanced in gentlemanly language and courtesy, in the spirit of Christian forbearance." To guard against a rupture of the Union, he recommended adjustment in the structure of the body politic to eliminate the grievances which, if left to flourish, might contaminate the whole organism: "We should carefully remember the importance of carefully guarding against incipient evil. Let us draw a lesson from other portions of the physical world. Would the delicate human constitution avert fell disease, the remedy must be applied when first appearances show themselves; no neglected symptoms must be allowed to proceed indicating an inflamed state, and lastly a destruction of organs designed to inhale the vital air. . . . Would the suffering patient avoid pain and anguish from the bruised limb, it is too late to repent negligence, or to recoil when the sharp knife of the skilled surgeon gleams over the operating table ready

[23]

to sever the gangrened portion as the last chance of saving the vitality of the rest. Would we arrest the spark about to consume our countless possessions, and perhaps destroy many human lives we must take it at the beginning, when the breath of a child could extinguish it, not when the raging elements have been fanned to a fury during the unnoticed hours of the night, and now send to the starry vault a lurid glare that strives to emulate heaven's radiant luminary, but only renders the surrounding darkness deeper. Would we save from ship' wreck the sinking vessel, we must, if possible, stop the first leak, before the mighty rush of waters threatens to sink the gallant craft, a vessel built, perhaps, of the strongest oak, framed by the best workmen, rigged with consummate skill, manned with a dauntless crew. A few pounds of oakum may suffice, as yet to save thousands of lives; but let the leak progress, let the hold fill, let the pumps choke. . . . and soon one wild and deathknell shriek will rise above the din of the storm, the crash of break' ing spars, the thunder's roar following the electric flash. Too late ascend to an offended Diety the prayers of those who knew not or obeyed not His immutable laws." Unless sound counsel prevail, he foresaw "fierce civil war, in which the horrors of Delhi would be surpassed; for here the curse of Cain would be realized—brother butchering brother—the bullet of the fa' ther reaching perhaps the heart of his only son."

This impassioned appeal was given no more consideration than that accorded other equally sound warnings. But at least Owen had registered his stand on the great question of the day, and it had not endeared him to the slavocracy. Though his popularity with the students continued unabated, he felt as out of place as an interventionist in an isolationist rally. In 1858 he liquidated his interests in the Western Military Institute and returned to New Harmony, the lodestone of all the Owens.

Upon his return to Indiana, employment was already waiting upon him, for his brother, David Dale, the state geologist, was eager to have him join a surveying expedition of the central part of the state. When David Dale died in 1860, Richard was appointed state geologist, and in that capacity he carried on the survey of Richmond, Greensburg, Lawrenceburg, Rising Sun, Madison, Bedford, Greencastle, Brazil, Highland, Daviss [sic], Martin, Vincennes and Princeton. His notebook covering these surveys is richly illustrated with drawings and sketches, and gives detailed information concerning the nature of the soil, the contour of the land, the types of trees and crops. Even as a geologist he could not renounce teaching, for during the evenings he conducted lectures wherever he happened to be stationed. Wherever he was, he was the geology department *en mission*. As a natural-born teacher he loved to share his information.

Chapter III

RECORD IN THE WAR BETWEEN THE STATES

THE violent disturbance of the War Between the States interrupted Richard Owen in the midst of his geological survey of Indiana. Having participated in the Mexican War, he felt a strong urge to engage in this one also. The Union needed men of his training and judgment, and no sooner had the conflict begun than Governor Morton of Indiana offered him a lieutenant-colonelcy in the Fifteenth Indiana Volunteers. He accepted. He and his regiment were among the early units to experience fighting. He participated in the Battles of Rich Mountain and Green Briers, West Virginia. Shortly afterwards he confronted Robert E. Lee at Cheat Mountain, and so well did he handle his men in these engagements that Governor Morton promoted him to the rank of full colonel.

But Colonel Owen's qualifications at the moment were in greater demand back in Indiana than they were on distant battlefields, for Governor Morton recalled him to raise the Sixtieth Indiana Volunteers. When this assignment was completed, he was placed in command of that regiment. His two sons, Captain Eugene and Lieutenant Horace, served under their father.

However, Colonel Owen's most significant service in the army was rendered as the commanding officer, from February 24 to May 26, 1862, of Camp Morton, a prison camp for Confederate soldiers in Indianapolis, Indiana.

Although the War Between the States had been brewing for some years before its inception, neither side had made any serious preparation for its prosecution, and certainly no provision for the care of prisoners. During the early months of the war no effort was made in the North to confine Confederate prisoners in prison camps; they were generally paroled on condition that they took an oath not to serve in field units until they should be exchanged for Northern prisoners held by the Confederate States. Prisoners with money were permitted to reside in hotels, provided they reported daily to military headquarters. Impecunious captives were allowed to secure employment and to use the wages for their own maintenance. Situations were solved entirely according to local conditions and the ingenuity of community leaders. A comprehensive plan was lacking.

While this method of handling captured opponents might possess humanitarian attributes, it was not suited to the prosecution of the determined and violent struggle that was ensuing. Army regulations were, therefore, invoked. They called for a commissary-general of prisoners under the supervision of the Quartermaster General. In July, 1861, Secretary of War Simon Cameron appointed Lieutenant-Colonel William E. Hoffman of the Eighth Infantry Division to the office of Commissary-General. He quickly selected a staff and developed a system for the administration of prison camps.

The Union record in the War Between the States before February, 1862, was a discouraging succession of delays, failures, and mistakes. But in that month a break appeared in the communiques, for on February 6 Fort Henry was captured by Union forces and ten days later Fort Donelson surrendered. General Halleck, eager to be relieved of his prisoners without detailing any of his men to guard them, telegraphed governors of nearby states asking the number of prisoners he might send them for detention. On February 17, 1862, Governor Morton replied, "We can take 3,000 if necessary." Five days later 3,700 Confederate prisoners arrived in the Hoosier capital.

Camp Morton until then had been an army training center for Union soldiers. The task of converting it to a prison camp for Confederate captives devolved upon Captain James A. Ekin, an assistant quartermaster general of the United States Army, who had been stationed in Indianapolis since the preceding August. In great haste he tore down the temporary shelters that had housed Union soldiers during the previous summer and reconstructed these into six dormitories and a mess hall, while additional structures were erected with lumber from vacated stables on the grounds.

Eighteen days after the arrival of the prisoners, Colonel Hoffman visited Camp Morton on a tour of inspection. After viewing the hastily erected barracks he reported that the quarters were "dark and close and there must be much sickness . . . unless some improvements are made." In consequence, the barracks were provided with windows for light and ventilation. The situation was further improved in June by the construction of still more barracks; but even so the hygienic conditions were not good.

The camp was surrounded by a wall built from two-inch oak planks. Four feet from the top on its outside a catwalk was built, along which the guards walked and from which they could observe the prison personnel and quell disturbances if and when they arose. The entrance gates were so reconstructed and re-enforced that concerted rushes by the prisoners would not demolish them. The sanitary problems of sewage and of water supply were solved. Latrines were so constructed and their sites so chosen that excrement and waste drained away from the camp at a point below the level of the springs supplying the camp with water.

The first consignment of prisoners arrived in Indianapolis on February 22, 1862. Within a few days additional trains

[28]

brought still more Confederates, who were quartered in Camp Morton or adjacent barracks. After confining the prisoners, the most urgent problem was that of providing them with food, for upon their arrival they were nearly famished. This task should have been executed by the Federal Commissary Department, but it had detailed no officer to meet this situation nor authorized anyone else to do so. Strict adherence to military regulations would have left the prisoners in desperate straits. Individual initiative and the United States Sanitary Commission, the forerunner of the United Service Organization, came to the rescue. Commissary-General Stone, of Governor Morton's staff, ordered about 4,000 rations at twenty-five cents each on his own authority and secured validation later. The prisoners arrived without adequate clothing, very few of them having blankets and still fewer overcoats. What clothing they did have was in serious disrepair. All of them, accustomed to the milder climate of Mississippi, Tennessee, and Kentucky, suffered from the colder weather of Indiana, and many of them contracted illnesses. These were despatched for treatment to local hospitals whose staffs were already overworked.

The situation improved within a few days after the arrival of the prisoners, for the United States Commissary Department sent blankets and other equipment which the army had rejected for regular army use because of flaws or other substandard qualities. Though these articles were below standard, they were cheerfully welcomed by the destitute men. The generosity of citizens also came to the rescue, for Hoosiers sent wagonloads of "necessaries and comforts and even the luxuries of life." The Indiana Adjutant General, Lazarus Noble, afraid that the charge would soon be made that the "Sesesh rebels" were better cared for than were Union soldiers in their army camps, in a letter to an inquiry defined what he considered should be the nature of the treatment accorded the prisoners: "Every attention will be paid to the Prisoners

[29]

that their necessities and well-being demand; anything further will not be allowed. They and their friends must reflect that they are Rebel Prisoners and as such cannot be allowed the luxuries and comforts incident to a peaceful home."

Enlisted men and officers were at first quartered together in Camp Morton; but this practice was soon abandoned, for officers instigated truculence and desertion in their subordinates. Separate quarters were therefore provided for the officers, who were housed in barracks on Washington Street east of the Odd Fellows Hall. Here they received the food and clothing to which they were entitled as prisoners of war; but since these meals did not satisfy Southern appetites, the officers ordered supplementary food from the nearby Palmer House. Immediately there were loud protests from Indianapolis citizens against the coddling of Confederate culinary idiosyncrasies at what they believed was public expense. These outcries were not silenced until it was explained that the cost of these indulgences was defrayed by General Simon B. Buckner, the captured Confederate commanding officer.

A more difficult problem was the guarding of the prisoners. As soon as the Governor was notified of the coming of Confederate captives, he summoned a number of partially filled regiments that were being enlisted throughout the state. Among these were the Fourteenth Battery of Light Artillery under Captain Meredith Kidd, the Fifty-Third Regiment of Indiana Volunteers under Colonel Walter Q. Gresham, and the Sixtieth Indiana Volunteers, all of which reached Indianapolis within a few days after the Governor's order had been issued. Colonel Ben S. Nicklin, the commanding officer of the camp until the arrival of the new regiments, was then relieved of his duties, which were assumed by Colonel Owen.

The camp was in this formative and unorganized condition when Colonel Owen was placed in command. Almost everything remained to be done, while precedents were lacking and directions from the War Department were general. The new commanding officer met the requirements of this situation remarkably well. He viewed his new assignment chiefly from the humanitarian point of view. He recognized that a major problem in readjustment was inescapable, and he aimed at facilitating its accomplishment with as little embarrassment and hardship to the men as was possible, without any sacrifice of the public interest. He was firm without being harsh, gentle without being weak, sympathetic without being sentimental. His primary object was to treat the prisoners in such a way as "to make them less restless in their confinement, and likely, when they returned to their homes, to spread among their friends and acquaintances the news that they had been deceived regarding northern men."

One of the first duties that devolved upon Colonel Owen was the formulation of a set of rules that should govern the conduct of the prisoners, and in this matter his superiors were more of a handicap than an aid. Colonel Hoffman, the commissary-general of prisoners, insisted that such matters should be left to his department; generals in the field were inclined to surrender their prisoners without releasing their authority over them; while the public in a wide-open frontier democracy believed that its wisdom could not safely be ignored. Adjutant-General Noble, on February 24, 1862, acting under orders of Governor Morton, had issued a few general regulations; but these were not sufficiently comprehensive for the care of 4,000 men. These orders merely stipulated that prisoners were to continue their former company organizations under the command of their highest ranking non-commissioned officer, and that they were to enjoy the same quality of food, clothing, and equipment as that granted to Indiana troops in the field. They were to be held incommunicado from civilians. Company rolls were to be kept.

The application of these rules still left a wide field of conduct that needed direction. To regulate that zone Colonel Owen drafted a set of regulations that defined the liberties and duties of the prisoners. They follow:

1. The entire camp prisoners will be divided into thirty divisions, each under charge of a chief selected by companies composing the division from among the first sergeants of companies. At the bugle call for first sergeants they will report themselves at headquarters.

2. These chiefs of divisions will draw up the provision returns for their divisions, care for and be responsible for the general appearance, police, and welfare of their divisions. The first fifteen will constitute a board of appeal for the hearing of grievances, settlement and punishment of misdemeanors, subject to the approval of the commander of the post in their fifteen divisions. The other fifteen will form a like court for the remaining fifteen divisions.

3. Among the crimes and misdemeanors against which first sergeants are expected to guard and which they will punish on detection are counterfeiting the commandant's, doctor's, adjutant's or chaplain's hands for requisitions, making improper use of premises, refusing to take a reasonable share in details according to the roster, selling to the sutler any articles issued to them as clothing, appropriating things belonging to others, or insulting sentinels.

4. The prisoners' returns will be handed in for approval at 10 a. m. each alternate day previous to the one on which the issue is made. The issues of tobacco and stationery will be made on Wednesdays and Saturdays at 2 p. m. by the chaplains, as well as the distribution of reading matter. Letters will be given out between 2 and 3 p. m. and mailed between 3 and 4 p. m.

5. Daily inspection will be made by the commandant of officers of the day to see that the policing so essential to health has been thoroughly performed, and facilities will be afforded for sports and athletic exercise also conducive to health as well as bathing by companies, if permission can be obtained by the proper authorities.

6. The first sergeants of their companies will look after the general wants of their companies and maintain the neces-

sary order, discipline and police essential to health and comfort, and will make requisitions, first on chiefs of divisions,
and they afterwards at headquarters, for clothing, camp and
garrison equipage absolutely necessary; also, for tobacco wanted
and the like.

7. The inside chain of soldiers, except a small patrol with
side-arms, will be removed, and the quiet and good order of
the camp as well as the policing for health and comfort, the
construction of new sinks when necessary and the daily throw-
ing in of lime and mold to prevent bad odors will be entirely
under the supervision of the sergeants of prisoners.

8. Vessels for washing of clothing and ropes for clothes
lines will be furnished, and no bed or other clothing will be
put on roof tops or fences.

9. Prisoners will carefully avoid interrupting sentinels in
the discharge of their duty, and especially will not curse them,
use abusive language or climb onto trees or fences, as the
sentinels are ordered to fire if such an offense occurs after
three positive and distinct orders to desist, even in day time.
At night only one warning will be given any one climbing
on the fence tops.

10. A prisoners' fund will be created by the deduction as
heretofore of small amounts from the rations of beef, bread,
beans, etc., a schedule of which will be placed at the commissary department. This fund will be used for the purchase
of tobacco, stationery, stamps and such other articles as the
chiefs of divisions may report, and which should be drawn on
requisitions handed in by first sergeants between 9 and 10 a. m.
each day.

11. Every endeavor will be made by the commandant to
give each and every prisoner as much liberty and comfort as
is consistent with orders received and with an equal distribution
of the means at disposal, provided such indulgence never leads
to any abuse of the privileges.

These rules reveal Colonel Owen's intrinsic faith in humanity. The common man, even in the enemy ranks, he believed could be trusted. He acted upon the supposition that
people would respond to fair treatment, and that they would
recognize the advantage of co-operation and mutual goodwill,

even between captive and captor. His own benevolence toward his prisoners was unmistakable, and this attitude he was able to convey to his wards, so that the confidence and goodwill which he had for them they reciprocated in full measure toward him. Almost immediately sectional and enemy barriers were obliterated and the boys from Mississippi, Tennessee, and Kentucky soon regarded their commanding officer not as a jailer, but as a charitably disposed benefactor. Nor did his superiors fail to appreciate the meritorious quality of his rules, for Colonel Hoffman incorporated most of their provisions in his instructions to other prison commandants throughout the Union. Richard, the son, had been able to evoke that spirit of fellowship between himself and his prisoners that Robert, the father, had engendered between himself and his laborers in New Lanark. Whether Richard had acquired this faculty through inheritance or through environment is of no consequence. It was there, and it worked.

Colonel Owen was more than a Hoosier Justinian spending his time drafting regulations. He was also a practical administrator who implemented his rules into action. Organization there had to be, and within two days after taking command he divided the prisoners into thirty divisions and designated the respective officers for the various functions connected with the operation of the camp. He required that each division maintain rolls of its members; and here his sense of· humor came to his rescue, for men with a capricious instinct and others with a criminal record assumed ridiculous names in order to bury their past. Because of this shifting of names by the prisoners, Colonel Owen never was able to establish an absolutely authentic roll of his camp.

Though the prisoners might adopt fictitious names, they demanded real food, "prepared the way it orter be." That culinary standard could be achieved only by meeting southern kitchen practices. Since the prisoners were accustomed to lean bacon, they inveighed against northern brands with alternating strips of lean and fat. They complained that the bread was sour and the meat all bone. They demanded "good cawn pone with the drippin's." Though they heaped abomination and ridicule upon their rations, they insisted upon their full and fair share. If by accident one prisoner was given a more generous serving than his buddies, there was an astonishing and unwarranted outburst of abuse and protest. And if the cooks did not guard the food with vigilance, the prisoners would launch a stampede for its capture with much of the fury of the Virginia cavalary against Little Round Top. Since rations were issued only once daily, prisoners at first partitioned it into three portions to be eaten at intervals during the day. But food thus reserved often fell victim to thievery, and as a consequence the rations were usually eaten when issued, or else prisoners concealed the food on their persons until hunger moved them to consume it. Colonel Owen met these problems with judgment and in a manner that reflected his faith in his fellow men. Most of the minor infractions of the camp rules he turned over to the prisoners for their own prosecution.

While Colonel Owen was in charge of Camp Morton he won the goodwill of his wards as few commanders in like positions have ever done. This he did by identifying his interest with the welfare of the prisoners, by convincing them of his benevolent purpose. Before his assumption of command and for some time thereafter, bread for the camp was purchased from commercial bakeries. Colonel Owen perceived that the profits exacted by the bakeries neither enlarged nor enriched the diet of the consumers. Furthermore, if the camp could establish its own bakery, the prisoners could furnish the labor involved in baking and thereby effect a saving, which revenue could be used to promote the comfort and welfare of the prisoners. This idea was also heartily endorsed by Colonel

Hoffman, and by the middle of April, 1862, a bakehouse went into operation. Within two weeks a fund of $2,400 had been accumulated. This fund defrayed the cost of "tobacco, stationery, stamps, wheelbarrows and tools for policing, scissors for cutting the hair, planks and nails for making bunks, lines for airing clothes, thread for repairs, etc., etc., also additional vegetables such as potatoes and onions, and some extra supply of molasses." This fund grew rapidly, and it was used to defray extra hospital expenses, to erect additional buildings, and to pay supplementary civilian employees. The prisoners were not unappreciative.

Colonel Owen promoted the well-being of the prisoners in other ways not demanded of him by military regulations. He co-operated harmoniously and cheerfully with the Patriotic Societies and the Sanitary Commission, which organizations provided the prisoners with many items that added comfort and cheer to these young men far from home. He approved their request for fresh straw for their bunks; he permitted them to receive supplies from home, although jams, jellies, and other delicacies were reserved for those confined in hospitals. He spared no effort to secure additional needed blankets and clothing, and so effective were his efforts that the prisoners registered few complaints on this score.

Almost simultaneously with the establishment of Camp Morton as a prison camp, Governor Morton issued an order prohibiting citizens or guards from conversing with the prisoners. This order prevented prisoners from receiving friends and relatives; yet, although Morton's order was published in the Louisville newspapers, devoted Kentuckians rushed northward to see their loved ones. Though great pressure was brought to bear upon Colonel Owen to interpret the Governor's order loosely, he scrupulously enforced Morton's instructions. In other prison camps throughout the North, visits from friends, some of whom were openly hostile to the Union, had stirred up a truculent unrest among the inmates. In such matters Colonel Owen's devotion to the Union took precedence over his loyalty to his wards. Governor Morton's and Colonel Owen's policy on this point was communicated to Secretary of War Stanton, who commended it highly and ordered restrictions tightened at other camps.

Nor did Colonel Owen permit an unrestricted use of the mails to the prisoners. A free flow of letters would have enabled them to order firearms and ammunition with which to effect their escape, or to secure articles which would have facilitated disturbance or riot. He therefore provided a system of censorship of all outgoing and incoming mail. He cheerfully enforced a federal order that limited letters written by prisoners to one page, whose content should be of a strictly private kind.

Colonel Owen at first imposed no regulation regarding the subject of money in the possession of the prisoners. Some of them had arrived with limited funds and others had received some gratuities from home after their confinement in the camp. Later, however, he came to the conclusion that prisoners were using some of their money for the purpose of bribery and that such use of it would inevitably foment trouble. After consultation on the subject, Adjutant-General Noble ordered that prisoners' money should be in the custody of the Commandant, who should surrender it to them as they might need it.

Colonel Owen's sense of humor saved him from retributive action against the author or the recipient of a doggerel from a Southern lassie who expressed her contempt of President Lincoln. She declared she would "be for Jeffdavise til the tenisee river freezes over, and then be for him, and scratch on the ice

> Jeffdavise rides a white horse,
> Lincoln rides a mule,
> Jeffdavise is a gentleman,
> Lincoln is a fule.

[37]

She gave further vent to her hostility toward Northerners by continuing: "I wish I could send them Lincoln devels some pies, they would never want any more to eat in this world."

Another problem that demanded Colonel Owen's attention was the presence of sutlers. The prices for commodities were in inverse ratio to their owners' morality, whose unscrupulousness was a fair index of their prosperity. To protect the prisoners' interests Colonel Owen constituted an Office of Price Administration and appointed himself its director. He designated Nathan Crawford camp sutler and ruled that thereafter small purchases should be made through him; Crawford was given a monopoly of the sale of small articles and was ordered to observe certain price ceilings.

"Tell me what you read, and I will tell you what you are" is a maxim that may have been coined before the War Between the States. But whether Colonel Owen had ever heard it or not, he applied its principle by supplying the prisoners with wholesome books that he secured from the superintendent of public instruction. His friends in New Harmony contributed numerous volumes for the soldiers, and these were offered not only because of the benefit they would be to the boys who read them, but also as a testimony of the high regard in which they held their "Richard" and the pleasure they experienced in promoting the success of his new responsibility. Colonel Owen also permitted certain designated persons to sell additional books and magazines to the prisoners, for as he said their reading would keep them "occupied and contented."

Though Colonel Owen forbade Southerners from seeing his prisoners, he raised no objection to prisoners' sending their photographs to their friends and relatives below the Mason and Dixon Line. He permitted his wards to go to a nearby "daguerrian" to have their pictures taken, but with the reservation that the photographer was to have no conversation with his subjects except that required for the transaction.

Another diversion to which Colonel Owen raised no objection was music. Though regulations forbade the prisoners from congregating in groups of any size, he nevertheless relaxed the rule to allow the formation of a number of glee clubs which entertained the men. A group of colored boys who had accompanied their masters sang minstrel songs. On one occasion the glee clubs took the liberty of serenading the officers of the camp with "Dixie" and other songs dear to Confederate hearts. Those who possessed dramatic ability were permitted to organize a theatrical troupe to present plays. The granting of such indulgences explains in a large measure why these men in later years remembered gratefully their former commandant.

Those who possessed neither musical nor dramatic ability were allowed to organize ball teams, while those who had no facility with the bat expressed their personality by carving or whittling. Thousands of simple articles soon graced the camp, and newsboys with a sharp eye for bargains quickly developed a brisk business in contraband goods. Such business enterprise could not escape the ears of Indianapolis citizens, who inquired about the equipment of the prisoner-artisans; upon being told that the carving had been done with knives, as they suspected, they expressed their surprise that Colonel Owen should have entrusted the prisoners with dangerous weapons. So many protests poured in upon the Commandant that he could silence them only by calling in the knives and other equipment that had been used in the whittling and carving pursuits. In each case Colonel Owen issued receipts for articles surrendered and returned them to the owners when they were exchanged or liberated.

Colonel Owen's devotion to the happiness of his prisoners was by no means cooled by public criticism, and so another outburst of denunciation was inescapable. For some time before the whittling and carving incident he had permitted

[39]

prisoners to visit their friends in the hospitals. Since there had been no abuse of this indulgence, he had permitted the men en route to purchase through their sergeants commodities of various kinds, on condition that there be no conversation with storekeepers except regarding the transaction. On one such occasion the men had started towards the business district and along their march had entered a saloon where their thirst exceeded their judgment. What was worse, their concern for their fellow prisoners was greater than their regard for prison rule, for they smuggled some of the firewater back to the barracks. A riot ensued, during which the hilarious prisoners pelted the sergeant of the guard with stones and beef bones. In self-defense and without authorization from Colonel Owen, the sergeant ordered his men to fire upon the boisterous prisoners. When the smoke had cleared away four prisoners were found injured, two so seriously that they were sent to the hospital. In the noise and disturbance, the battery of light artillery commanding the camp opened fire with blank cartridges. In the meantime Colonel Owen appeared, but by that time the vapor from the alcohol-fogged intellects had dissipated and the prisoners were regarding their Bacchanalian folly in a repentant mood.

The Commandant was not the only one aroused by the camp commotion. The incident became a subject of community concern, and Governor Morton demanded an explanation. Indianapolis newspapers, reflecting the exasperation of the community, were extremely critical of Colonel Owen for so running the camp that such an incident should happen.

Colonel Owen, on the following day, April 16, met the criticism with courage, frankness, and force. He revealed the conditions under which the group had been allowed to go to the hospital, and said that since those terms had been violated by the prisoners, similar privileges for the future had been suspended. He declared that he had been unable to ascertain who had thrown the rocks at the guards, but added that the prisoners had assured him that they would discover the guilty and bring them to justice. With dignity he informed Governor Morton that if his services were not satisfactory, he would welcome the opportunity to surrender his post, and that his regiment would relish a change in assignment. He reminded the Governor of the high mortality among his troops although they were only doing guard duty, and of the fact that for the past six months he had received no compensation for his services.

To mollify the public he wrote an article on April 17, 1862, in the Indianapolis *Journal,* in which he set forth his principles for running the camp and in general how fully the objectives had been realized. Lest anyone should suppose that his responsibilities were light, he stated that his duty had kept him at his post almost continuously and that since his assignment at Camp Morton he had not spent a single night away from his quarters, that he had never entered a saloon or a hotel, and that on numerous nights, in order to be ready for any emergency, he had not even removed his uniform. He justified his command of the camp by saying that, though he had 4,200 prisoners under his care, only thirteen had escaped and that some of these had been apprehended and returned.

Incidents such as these might momentarily diminish Colonel Owen's confidence in his prisoners; yet fundamentally he believed in their good faith and, acting upon it, he extended new privileges. As the warm May days fell upon Indiana, the prisoners experienced nostalgic visions of the swimming holes in Mississippi, Tennessee, and Kentucky, and requested permission to swim in Fall Creek. Colonel Owen's kindly and sympathetic nature could not deny them this indulgence, and, in consequence, small groups of men were taken daily under guard to the river. On one of these trips a group of prisoners asked their guards if they might inspect the new

Enfield rifle. With some want of judgment the guards surrendered their weapons, and in a flash the prisoners were pro-
ceeding at double time toward the region of magnolias, cane,
and cotton. Thereafter Colonel Owen enforced a stricter guard
system, and, in consequence, escapes from Camp Morton no-
ticeably decreased.

One of the most difficult problems imposed upon Colonel
Owen was the passing of judgment upon various petitions received by him. These were of every variety, although most
of them concerned requests for parole. His reactions to these
requests reveal his sterling character. When humanitarianism
could be served without jeopardy to the Union, he was inclined
to give the petitions a sympathetic consideration; but there is
no evidence to indicate that he ever betrayed his trust or com-
promised his character. One petitioner requested to be re-
leased "without arousing any suspicion" and four members of
a fraternal organization of which he was a member promised
that if Colonel Owen would parole the prisoner, they would
never divulge the fact. Colonel Owen's rejection of such propo-
sitions was tinged with anger.

Whatever excitement attended Colonel Owen's administration of the camp was always of minor importance, and it is a
tribute to his powers of management that a harmonious relationship existed within the camp and between it and the surrounding citizenry.

The serenity prevailing in this prison camp was in sharp
contrast to the conflict in 1862 between the Union and Confederate forces. Lee was exerting strong pressure on Northern
lines, and this led Secretary of War Stanton to call for additional men from all over the country to resist the Southern
surge. Consequently, on May 26, 1862, orders were sent out
by the War Department for the transfer of the Sixtieth Indiana Volunteers (Owen's regiment) to Halleck's command.
It would have been possible perhaps to leave Colonel Owen in

command of Camp Morton; but as Governor Morton and Colonel Hoffman wanted to retain the organization of the regiment intact, the Colonel accompanied his men on their new assignment. And Colonel Owen, certainly, raised no objection to active service on the firing line.

His administration of Camp Morton had been highly appreciated by his superiors, for Colonel Hoffman, on an inspection tour of Camp Morton late in May, 1862, expressed high commendation of all the departments of the camp as well as of Colonel Owen's management of the prisoners. Even Secretary of War Stanton, who was not given to idle flattery, pronounced Camp Morton, while under Owen's command, one of the best administered prison camps in the whole country. The most touching manifestation of esteem, however, came from the prisoners whom he had been guarding. When they learned of the order for his transference, they drew up the following petition requesting his retention as commanding officer of the camp:

Knowing that it is a matter of state pride with your Exellency that prisoners of war sent to Indiana should remain quietly until satisfactory arrangments can be made for their release, and believing that this object can better be attained by the 60th Regiment being retained in their present situation than by any change, we respectfully solicit your Excellency, if not inconsistent with the interests to which you are pledged, that you will permit the same regiment to remain in command of Camp Morton feeling that while true to their Government and strictly carrying out all regulations of your Excellency, they have combined therewith the humanity and kindness we so highly appreciate. As an inducement to grant our request we pledge ourselves that we will conform to the prescribed rules and regulations adopted by your Excellency for our observation and safe keeping, and you will never have to repent your having granted us this favor.

Since Governor Morton, however, felt under greater obligation to obey Stanton's orders than to grant the request of

Confederate prisoners, Colonel Owen was sent to the front. On June 20, 1862, he and his regiment left Indianapolis for Louisville. From there they were sent to Lebanon and then to Munfordville, Kentucky, where they were surrounded by Confederates under General Bragg and then taken prisoners. Some of his former students of the Kentucky Military Institute, then fighting for the Confederacy, at first gloated over the news that "Old Dick and both his boys" had been caught. But with all their satisfaction over his discomfiture they shielded him from harm, and rejoiced when General Buckner, one of the Confederate generals, personally called on Colonel Owen and expressed his appreciation of the kindness that Colonel Owen had shown the prisoners at Camp Morton. When the Sixtieth Indiana Regiment was paroled, Colonel Owen was given his full liberty and allowed to retain his sidearms. General B. R. Johnston, with whom he had been associated as teacher, and two former students whom Colonel Owen had often drilled, but who were now officers in the Confederate army, called on him. General Bragg, whose acquaintance he had made in the Mexican War, also paid his respects and showed him conspicuous courtesy.

Marked as were these manifestations of esteem, the enduring regard of his former prisoners more touchingly expressed itself half a century after their detention in Camp Morton. As the fiftieth anniversary of their imprisonment approached, Mr. S. A. Cunningham, editor of the *Confederate Veteran,* proposed that a memorial be erected to the memory of Colonel Richard Owen. The suggestion met with a hearty response. Immediately contributions converged from all directions upon the office of the *Confederate Veteran,* many of them accompanied by testimonials to Colonel Owen's kindness. The few hundred remaining veterans who had been under Colonel Owen's command at Camp Morton agreed to express their appreciation by placing a bronze bust of him in the State

House of Indiana. In June, 1913, amid impressive ceremonies, attended by Vice-President Marshall, the Governor and Mrs. Ralston, Miss Belle Kinney, the sculptress of the bust, Mr. S. A. Cunningham, and many other distinguished men and women, General Bennett H. Young, Commander of the United Confederate Veterans, presented the bust of Colonel Richard Owen to the State of Indiana. In doing so he said, "There is no monument in this state that can reflect higher honor on the people of Indiana, or that in ages to come will tell of a nobler, gentler, more heroic spirit than that of him to whose memory we tender this tribute of gratitude and love. Brave in war, honorable in peace, cultured in mind and magnanimous of soul, he demonstrated in the face of opposition and censure that while he was a patriotic soldier, he was yet a true man, and filled with the loftiest instincts of generosity and mercy. . . ." In response Vice-President Marshall said that the "spectacle of prisoners of war paying such a tribute to their captor is one without precedent in history and one which should be an inspiration to the people of the United States. . . ."

In 1933, through the efforts of President Edward C. Elliott of Purdue University and President William Lowe Bryan of Indiana University, replicas of the bust were cast, and one was placed in the Union Building of Indiana University and another in that of Purdue University.

Shortly after Colonel Owen's capture, he was paroled; and as soon as an exchange could be arranged he was allowed to return to the Northern armies. He was immediately assigned to the army of Tennessee and later detailed to the Arkansas region. He participated in the taking of Arkansas Post, where his regiment lost heavily and many soldiers in his immediate vicinity were either killed or wounded. He and his regiment fought with Grant at Vicksburg until its surrender. He also fought with Sherman at the capture of Jackson, Mississippi. Subsequently Colonel Owen and his troops were ordered to join the forces of General Banks in the Red River campaign. In one of these battles, Carrion-Crow Bayou, he was in full command of a brigade, and apparently he was on the threshold of larger responsibilities.

But Colonel Owen decided not to embrace opportunities that might be waiting for him in the army. Earlier in the year (1863) his son, Horace, who was an adjutant of a brigade, had resigned his commission to return to civilian life in order to care for his mother. Colonel Owen did not want to shift indefinitely the responsibility on the son which in reality was his own. Furthermore, Colonel Owen was not primarily a military man. Intellectually he convinced himself that the Union could be maintained only by a costly sacrifice of blood and treasure, and he was willing to be an instrument in that grim game as long as the situation remained critical. But by the end of 1863 Vicksburg and Gettysburg were in Union hands, the back of the South had been badly strained if not broken, and the prospect of Northern victory seemed assured. Consistent and cautious effort applied against the South, he believed, was the essential prescription of victory. He realized that others could render that service as well as himself, and his loyalty to the country had been attested by service in two wars.

Civilian life appealed to him more strongly than to most people. He was primarily a scholar, a philosopher, and a humanitarian, and when Indiana University offered him a professorship in the natural sciences, he put away the military toga and donned the academic gown. On January 1, 1864, he took up his residence at Bloomington, Indiana, and began his teaching career there, which continued until his retirement in 1879, after fifteen distinguished years.

Chapter IV

PROFESSOR AND CITIZEN

N JANUARY 1, 1864, Owen unbuckled his sword and donned academic attire. He changed his title from colonel to professor as he assumed his teaching duties at Indiana University. He was then fifty-four years of age. Teaching was, however, no new experience for him. Years of soldiering and surveying had merely interrupted his main pursuit. As a young man he had taught elementary school children; for nine years he had taught at Western Military Institute. While he had been on geological surveys, he had lectured on various subjects to the citizens among whom he had carried on his work. Somewhat like Lincoln, he yearned to impart his knowledge to others. His academic training, as well as his experience, qualified him as a teacher. His schooling at Hofwyl and at Andersonian Institute had been thorough; his continued research with his brother, Dale, had sharpened his scholarship, and his studies leading to a degree in medicine had broadened his information. Most important of all, Professor Owen never relaxed his mental activity. Though he was professor for fifteen years, he was a student all his life. He enjoyed learning for learning's sake and, when he faced his classes in 1864, he was a man of mature scholarship. His speeches and writings reveal a wide acquaintance with many fields of literature.

Indiana University was not a large institution when Professor Owen began his teaching there. In 1863, there were 112 students in the collegiate department and 96 in the preparatory school. The collegiate staff comprised seven professors, most of whom had been connected with the University in 1853, at which time "all save the president were scholarly men." Professor Owen did not lower the intellectual caliber; he was soon classified with the superior group, which became known as the "Big Four." They were Professors Ballantine, Kirkwood, Wylie, and Owen.

Professor Owen's mastery of his subject matter was indisputable. What is more important, he possessed a philosophy of education that gave tone and color to his teaching. It made him a teacher of men as well as of subject matter. At his own request the epitaph on his tombstone is: "His first desire was to be virtuous, his second to be wise." He was wont to remark, "The sum of wisdom is to know the laws of nature by which the universe is governed; the sum of virtue is to obey them." His ruling passion as a teacher was to qualify others to merit his own epitaph by unfolding for them the secrets of nature. And he took his responsibilities seriously, almost as conscientiously as a monk directing novitiates.

With a nineteenth-century ecclesiastical view of education, he implored every fellow-teacher to exercise a watchful care "over the health, the mental development and the moral purity of those entrusted to his charge or coming more immediately under his supervision in his classes, learning to view them as he would his own near and dear relatives, realizing further the solemn truth aroused by a sense of the educator's responsibility to God and our country for the immortal soul consigned to our care; the position of the instructor, rightfully viewed, may become one of pleasure; correctly appreciated by parents, should be one of reasonable profit to the instructor and judiciously pursued should evidently impress us as one of high responsibility.

"In view of these facts let us not be satisfied with barely performing our duties and obtaining a commercial equivalent,

SOLDIER

PROFESSOR

THE BUST BY BELLE KINNEY

but let us dignify the profession that students shall love to sit beneath our instruction and give heed to our admonition, that parents shall confide to us their jewels with abiding trust, that God Himself shall approve and shall pour out upon us a double portion of His Holy Spirit, sanctifying us to mold the future citizen of this glorious republic for such health of body, vigor of intellect, elevation in morality, purity in spirituality that all the nations of the earth shall through them respect her power, pay tribute to her intellect, commend her unwavering virtue, and imitate her obedience to human and divine law."

While this may seem like an extravagant delineation of duty, Professor Owen did not miss his own ideal very far. A large number of former students attest his scholarship, character, and nobility of soul. Mrs. Emma Jennings Clark, of the class of 1873, seventy-one years after attending his classes still remembers him as an "excellent teacher and noble gentleman." Mr. Charles F. Carpenter, another surviving student, says that Professor Owen "was unquestionably master of his subject matter. Evolution was a new doctrine; Darwin, Huxley, and Tyndall were living then, and he was abreast of their work. His deep reverence for truth resembles that of Kepler bowing in awed humility and saying, 'I am thinking thy thoughts after thee, O God.' And we students, surrounded by thousands of forms of life, beheld through his eyes the epic of creation unfolding. To me Dr. Owen was hero, sage and friend." Dr. William Lowe Bryan, though never a student of Professor Owen, knew him well and admired him deeply. Professor Owen infused in students not only an appreciation of his subject matter, but also an affection for himself. Nor did his colleagues fail to appreciate his high qualities. The late David Starr Jordan observed him as "a gentle and reverent man, unassuming and unselfish in all his relations. A man of perfect courtesy of thought: a man whom everybody loved because his love went out to everybody. He was the highest type of teacher, of naturalist, of scholar, of soldier even, because above all he was the highest type of man." The same nobility of soul, excellence of character, and simplicity of manner that impressed the Confederate prisoners at Camp Morton left their mark upon his students and associates. Knowledge of subject matter is an important qualification in a teacher. Character, whose traits are conveyed more by example than by precept, is no less essential in a leader of youth. Judged by either standard, Professor Owen met the full requirements.

As a classroom manager he was superb. He maintained an atmosphere of dignity and scholarship. Raucous hilarity springing from demagogic stimuli was entirely absent. To him the classroom was not a place for entertainment, light bantering, or exhibition of the instructor's personality, but rather for the revelation of a theory or the exposition of a principle. He held that the quest for knowledge is sufficiently intriguing to scorn tawdry appeals; the consciousness of conquest, sufficiently inspiring to drive the students in search of new triumphs.

This devotion to scholarship and ideals did not make him aloof and remote, for Professor Owen was full of human sympathy. To him the members of the class did not appear as did Queen Victoria to Gladstone, a public department, but rather as she did to Disraeli, a woman, a personality. Bright students with an inquiring mind eagerly lingered after class for further discussion of the subject under consideration, and none of them left without having peered a little farther into the unknown. Nor did he ignore those who had scholastic difficulties. In 1913 Senator Newell Sanders of Tennessee remarked that "Dr. Owen was especially kind and helpful to those of us who were from the country and behind in our studies." The human touch was not missing. Indeed, if the occasion demanded it he could "use his temper, and not lose it."

Extant outlines reveal that he made careful preparation for his class meetings. Long before pedagogues advised the use of lesson plans, Professor Owen organized his discussions into introduction, motivation, body, and conclusion. He rarely used the lecture method; he placed his confidence in discussions. He made generous use of charts to illustrate his discussions. These covered the walls and boards of his classroom and presented to the eye the geological formation of the earth as well as the classification of animal and vegetable kingdoms. He also adorned his room with the busts of the great scientists: Cuvier, Audubon, Linnaeus, Huxley, Tyndall, and others; and their names and those of many others frequently were referred to during the class hour.

When he was first engaged to teach at Indiana University, he had agreed to offer instruction in geology, chemistry, and natural philosophy. In 1873, owing to the shortage of modern language teachers, and to his competence in German and French, he began teaching in these fields also. Years spent at Hofwyl had fortified him for such an emergency.

As a teacher he manifested a lively interest in his subject matter. His absorption in what he was teaching was so complete that only one who believed that his auditors shared his fervor could have sustained so high a pitch of enthusiasm. And yet his ardor revealed no excitability, but rather a total engrossment. His immersion in whatever he was teaching was so entire that he assumed that all his students followed with an equal zeal; or perhaps he was so aglow with what he was doing that he did not observe any attitude to the contrary. At any rate he did not try to compel any attention by arbitrary technique. He marshalled a fund of information and interpretation, opened new avenues of thought; and students who desired to profit by it were welcome to anything he had to offer. Those who preferred to meditate upon the last class rush or election, he did not disturb. He was not the drill-master.

An old student device to escape responsibility for an assign-ment is to sidetrack the discussion to the professor's special field of interest. Indiana students three-quarters of a century ago practiced this universal guile, and Professor Owen was pe-culiarly susceptible to it. Even before he arrived in the United States he had traveled considerably upon the European con-tinent, and he was of course conversant with England, Wales, and Scotland. In 1869 he traveled in Europe and the Near East. He loved to relate his experiences in foreign lands and to describe distant countries. With appropriate conscientious-ness, he would open a discussion of the day's assignment only to be interrupted by a laggard whose object was to seek safety from pointed questions rather than information in Professor Owen's special hobby. Inquiries regarding the rock formations of Palestine or the Peloponnesus, the relative merits of Grant and Lee as strategists, and the most recent geological surveys by the instructor usually insured immunity from searching questions for forty to fifty minutes. This game with variations was played by the students *ad infinitum*.

Whether he spoke on curricular or extracurricular subjects, there was no disorder in his classes. His treatment of any subject was usually so engaging that it held the student's at-tention. Furthermore, a noble and dignified personality did not generate an atmosphere hospitable to frivolity.

Even during a period when the pressure to publish scarcely existed, Professor Owen wrote, not from any external com-pulsion but rather from an inner urge. In 1864 he made a geological survey of New Mexico and Arizona, and the report of this reconnaissance was published in the following year. In 1867 he made a similar survey of North Carolina. The report of this survey glows with prophecies of great opportunities: "Most excellent iron can be manufactured from magnetic iron ore, the iron rendered more valuable by the presence of tungs-ten." He believed that the Blue Ridge had large deposits of of gold, quartz, and copper, and that rich deposits of porcelain clay existed in both states. He predicted that, with the completion of the railroads in the area, prospects were good for the development of marble quarries. "As regards the agricultural facilities," he wrote, "I think it would be difficult to find a region which combines more advantages than are to be realized in the Blue Ridge tracts—pure water, extensive grazing range, proximity to market and fine scenery." He was most impressed by the agreeable climate, which he compared to the disadvantage of every other section of the country. The price of the land there, he asserted, was from $1 to $2 an acre, as compared to as much as $10 in other areas no better for settlement. He strongly recommended the section to prospective settlers.

In 1864 there appeared an article on "The Rock Salt of New Iberia," Louisiana, in the *Transactions of the St. Louis Academy of Science, Vol. II.* Other papers of his were published in the reports of the *American Association for the Advancement of Science,* the *Scientific American,* and the *American Meteorological Journal.* Even while he was contributing to these professional periodicals he also sought a wider reading public in the popular periodicals of his time as well as in the larger daily and weekly papers, including the *New York Tribune.* Less well-known papers to which he contributed were the *Indianapolis Journal,* the *Indiana Farmer,* and the *Evansville Journal.* He also published a series of articles in the *Southwestern Journal of Education* (Nashville) detailing some observations not found in physical geography. To these he gave the title: "Aids to the study of Geography." During his European tour in 1869 he published a series of fifteen letters, which appeared in the *Evansville Journal* (Indiana). Other letters were published in the *New York Tribune.*

Professor Owen's style was both facile and versatile. His articles in professional journals were scholarly and commanded the respect of the ablest readers; those written for popular consumption were characterized by sweeping generalizations and comprehensive conclusions. He was an artist of simplification. The causes and characteristics of earthquakes were discussed in the vernacular of the market place; in describing the influence of geography upon society he combined the verve of a realtor's talk and the integrity of a scholar's exposition. The reports of his geological surveys reveal the analysis of the scientist and the vision of the sociologist.

Professor Owen's activities were not confined to the classroom, for on January 29, 1864, less than a month after he took up his residence at Bloomington, he was chosen secretary to the faculty. This may have been a questionable honor, for it involved duties whose execution could scarcely produce claims to distinction. Professor Kirkwood, the retiring secretary, was no doubt glad to surrender the post to the academic recruit. And yet Professor Owen's performance of these duties was executed with fidelity and dignity until 1872, when he resigned as secretary, because he wanted to devote his time to the improvement of his own department. As secretary he drafted resolutions and petitions in gracious English, and he wrote condolences and congratulations in dignified diction. Nor were his services completely unappreciated, for upon the cessation of these responsibilities, the faculty passed a resolution commending his "courtesy, energy, and high Christian character worthy of appreciation."

On January 13, 1864, less than two weeks after his arrival on the campus, the faculty appointed him to "prepare some suggestions in regard to securing a geological cabinet and otherwise promoting the interests of the University." The geological collection referred to comprised the specimens gathered, largely, by David Dale Owen. In 1864 it contained more than 85,000 items and was valued at more than $50,000. These rock specimens exemplified the stones and fossils typical of western

[54]

Europe and the United States. Many of them were so arranged as to reveal the order of rock superimposition of the various geological epochs. Other arrangements displayed the specimens in the order of their luster, hardness, or cleavage.

In 1861 the Owen family, through Richard, had offered this collection for sale to the state of Indiana for $25,000. No action was taken on the matter until the faculty's appointment of Professor Owen to consummate the purchase. Upon his recommendation a special hall was constructed in which the collection was housed. There for many years it enriched his teaching; but unfortunately a fire in 1883 destroyed the building and most of the rock exhibits, as well as the catalogue of the contents.

Professor Owen was of value to the University in other ways. Upon the resignation of faculty members the President relied upon his judgment in the selection of new incumbents. When a new University code was drafted in 1872, it was largely the work of Professor Owen. When calls came to the University for speakers throughout the state, he was minute man with a battery of addresses ready for delivery at a moment's notice, for he was a versatile platform performer. He took an active part in the encampments of the Grand Army of the Republic; he frequently gave the main address in the state meetings of the Independent Order of Odd Fellows, of which organization he was a member; no Masonic meeting, to which organization he also belonged, was quite complete without his presence. Few professors anywhere in Indiana had as many contacts throughout the state as did he, and few could have represented the University so well.

A project of greater interest to him was the location of the land-grant college provided for by the Morrill Act of 1862. He had not been at Indiana University one month before the faculty passed a resolution designating President Nutt and Professor Owen "a committee to attend on behalf of the faculty, to securing if circumstances permit the establishment of the proposed Agricultural and Normal School in connection with the Indiana University, and report from time to time." Professor Owen took this assignment seriously, so seriously that he failed to attend faculty meetings because of "Agricultural College business." Shortly thereafter he was appointed to another faculty committee, composed of President Nutt, Professor Hoss, and himself, to confer with the County Commissioners to induce the location of the Agricultural College at Bloomington. Largely through Owen's persuasive powers the County Commissioners offered to appropriate $50,000 in order to locate the College at Bloomington, Indiana. Professor Owen traveled and spoke throughout the state in favor of selecting the University site for the proposed college.

He did more than that. He drafted a comprehensive plan for the organization of such an institution. It was to be situated upon a model farm of one hundred acres laid out in ten-acre plots. In the exact center of this farm was to be a model garden of ten acres. Dispersed around this plot were to be the nine fields of equal size but of various shapes to afford surveying students experience in their pursuit. In these fields the following crops were to be raised according to a definite system of rotation: (1) grass, (2) clover, (3) wheat, (4) barley, rye, or oats, (5) corn, (6) flax, (7) hemp, (8) a root crop, (9) fruit.

Special emphasis was to be given to the garden. It was to be fenced with posts placed at intervals of one rod, or one-half, in order to train the students in measuring distances. Special posts, higher than others, were to be set at intervals of one hundred yards, one hundred feet, fifty feet, etc., etc. For similar reasons pieces of ground were to be laid off so as to show the size of two acres, one acre, etc., etc. In this garden were to be cultivated all the useful and ornamental fruits.

[56]

He proposed to organize the instructional work of the college into eight departments, i. e., chemistry, languages, history, mathematics, natural history, music, drawing, and military tactics. Heads of departments were to be paid $1,500 a year, and the "adjunct professors," $1,000 a year. The estimated instructional budget for one year came to $19,000.

Professor Owen drafted minute regulations for the operation of each department. Foreign languages were to be learned through the conversational method, and not by memorizing innumerable rules, "usually forgotten before their practical application is called for." Under the department of mathematics he grouped physical geography and meteorology, and for this department as well as for all others he enumerated extensive lists of materials as instructional aids. These revealed a wide range of information outside his own field. For the agricultural section he recommended displays of the best implements and machinery, models of steam engines, water-wheels, dams and bridges, cotton and woollen milling equipment, etc., etc. On the farm should be samples of every important forest tree; in the farm museum should be specimens of every kind of wood. All the different varieties of seeds should be exhibited. His scheme provided for no engineering department, no doubt because eighty years ago differentiation was not as essential as it is today.

The cost of the physical plant for such an institution he reckoned at $200,000. This sum would cover the cost of a main building as well as an annex, a chapel, a laboratory, and faculty homes valued at $2,500 each, and those for the head gardener and farmer at $2,000 each.

He estimated that Congress would grant Indiana 390,000 acres of land, which if sold would yield $300,000, a sum greater than the initial cost of erecting the institution.

The institution should require no tuition fees. Selection of four students from each of Indiana's ninety-two counties every two years would assure an enrollment of 368. Characteristically, as one of the Owens, who were deeply moved by humanitarian impulses, he recommended the establishment of a school for Civil War orphans in connection with the agricultural college. And in harmony with Owen practicality, these children as well as the collegiate students should spend part of their time laboring on the college farm, under the direction of the head gardener and the head farmer. Those professors who desired to improve their physical health and energies might be provided with pitchfork or ax. Golf clubs were not included as essential equipment in a frontier agricultural college.

The farm crops were to be consumed right on the campus, for the orphaned children should not only be gratuitously instructed but also gratuitously boarded out of the profits of the farm and garden. Unmarried professors and students who took their meals at the college boarding house should pay for them on the basis of a fair price.

The influence of the father had not been lost on his youngest son, for Professor Owen recommended the establishment of nursery and kindergarten schools, where mothers could be relieved of their children by day, and where youngsters might play in well-arranged grounds and gardens under competent direction. Though he recognized childhood and infancy as important periods in an individual's life, he cautioned against the imposition of intellectual strain on young minds.

This in brief was the first conception of Purdue University. It was by no means the preview of what the university has become in its physical aspect; but it foretold the spiritual and intellectual nature of the institution which, from its site on the banks of the Wabash, radiates tolerance, enlightenment, and scientific discoveries.

Professor Owen pursued many projects and imparted to each the enthusiasm that most people reserve for their main activity. Besides teaching, advising the President on appointments, drafting plans for a new institution, he found time to carry on research. This study was confined chiefly to the field of geology. He did extensive work in detecting and predicting earthquakes. He demonstrated by means of the galvanometer the existence of thermo-electric currents in the earth's crust, which he revealed ran from east to west in the southern, and from south to north in the northern, hemisphere. He also constructed an electrical globe to demonstrate and explain the declination of the compass. Papers bearing on these subjects and terrestrial magnetism as related to the dynamics of geology were read at several meetings of the American Association for the Advancement of Science, and were also published in various periodicals, the *Scientific American,* the *American Polytechnical Review,* the *Transactions of the Academy of Sciences* at St. Louis, the Yale College *Courant,* the *Reports of the Department of Agriculture* at Washington, and the *Tennessee Farmer.* He also published papers on rainfall, the preservation of timber, the cause of Indian summer, and other subjects connected with physical geography. He investigated the flying weevil and published the results in the *Albany Cultivator.*

Satisfaction with one's achievements—resting on one's laurels —is the first evidence of intellectual disintegration. Professor Owen knew that when one does not go forward he goes backward, and to maintain the forward motion he pursued an active program of reading. His diary covering his teaching period contains several entries every week of books which he had read.

Further to stimulate his intellectual processes, he secured a year's leave of absence in 1869 to travel in Europe and the Near East. He went to England, visited his childhood surroundings, and renewed family friendships. He arrived in London on August 3, 1869, and enjoyed its sights. He discoursed on geological subjects with his namesake, Sir Richard Owen.

From there he went to the continent, revisited Hofwyl, dear to the hearts of all the Owens, and journeyed down the Danube to the Crimea and the Black Sea. At Sevastopol, Balaklava, Simferopol, and other places he collected geological specimens. He gathered basalt on the Bosporus, souvenirs in Constantinople, specimens of the bones of the *hipparion* in Athens, and other items at each point of his travels. He visited Nazareth, Beirut, and Damascus. He experienced a revivification of his spiritual zeal as he walked where Christ had labored. While in Jerusalem he met Emperor Francis Joseph of Austria-Hungary and the Crown Prince of Prussia, who were enroute to the opening of the Suez Canal. He attended the reception at Port Said for the royal representatives of the various nations.

Upon his arrival in the Holy Land he wrote his wife, "But most interesting of all was the sight of Gethsemane
the church which stands over the supposed spot of the tomb of our Savior." Faithful and devout believer that he was, he nevertheless wrote, "Regarding the Mt. of Olives and Geth-semane there can be no doubt, as well as about the situation of the Temple, but when they show you the Temple of the (Trojin) and the House of Pilate, the exact spot where Stephen was martyred, and the stone which was rolled from the sepulchre, you cannot help doubting; and when they undertake to exhibit the stone on which the cock stood when it crowed, after Peter denied our Lord, and similar relics, we are disgusted and mortified." From Jerusalem he traveled to Damascus and Samaria and then to Paris, thence to England and Scotland, and then finally back to Indiana University in 1870. Accounts of new experiences and varied geological specimens and visits with distinguished Europeans enlivened the treatment of his class discussions.

The man with constructive imagination is either honored as a genius or ridiculed as a fool. By the shallow-minded, Pro-fessor Owen was classified in the latter group because he strung fine cords over part of the Indiana University campus. He arranged his students in a circle clasping hands and then tested the circuit for electrical currents, first without moistening the hands of the students, then after they had inserted them in a strong saline solution. The unintelligent made no effort to ascertain the reason for the activity, and if they had been apprised of the object, they would have held him in still lower regard. He deserved better. He had divined the existence of ether waves and he was trying to prove their reality. He was endeavoring to catch their vibration even when Heinrich Rudolph Hertz (1857-1894) was still in his teens and Guglielmo Marconi (1874-1937) was entertaining himself with kindergarten toys. Had he been able to devote all his time to research, perhaps his name might have been identified with wireless telegraphy and radio.

Though some may have regarded his experiments as ludicrous, the Wabash College faculty and trustees appreciated his ability and contribution. In 1875 that institution conferred the degree of LL.D. upon him. The Scientific Association of Louisiana elected him to honorary membership.

Though he was deeply interested in science, he did not pursue its investigation to the exclusion of religion. During many years of residence in Bloomington, Indiana, he conducted a Sunday school class in the Presbyterian Church. His extant outlines reveal that he prepared for these sessions with the same care that he did for his secular courses. His class developed into a discussion group, which considered a variety of topics, such as religion, morality, economics, politics, ethics, frivolity, and family relations. From verbal exchanges on such topics it is obvious that he was permeated with a deep spirituality. He did not dispute or oppose the Supreme Will, but accepted with resignation the dictates of the Almighty: "Why Omnipotence chose to create man so that he might under certain circumstances err, or why God should create man at all, knowing that he would err, is not for the creature to ask. A Creator who has made a universe, every portion of which, as far as man

[61]

can understand it, is perfection—he would certainly not fail in His crowning work—the creation of man. Therefore, man, a being unable to prolong his existence one moment beyond the period assigned by the Almighty, . . . would exhibit con- summate ignorance and presumption to ask why God had made him . . . ."

To Richard Owen, God was a stern but loving and merciful judge. Men were wayward, but fortunately God was indulgent if only mortals recognized His supremacy: "People may not understand the mysteries of the compass, but they know that reliance on it has brought many a ship into port . . . So too the Christian may observe that many an anxious soul has been guided to a haven of rest by the teachings of the Scrip- tures." To him immortality was assured, "for that which we crave is given," and God has assured us that "our earthly bodies are converted into dust, but that our spirits are immortal and consigned either to happiness or misery."

Calvinist that he was, he demanded observance of the com- mandments. The Sabbath should not be used for "junketing" or even public social amusements, "but it should be devoted to consecration and prayerful thankfulness for God's prosperous mercies." Religion was to him a source of comfort. Observ- ance of its demands and compliance with its principles were not added burdens but aids to serenity and composure. His faithful observance of Christian principles may perhaps in part account for the absence of a single note of irritation among the hundreds of entries in his diaries. His own spirituality enabled him to comfort others; consequently, he was frequently asked to con- duct funeral services.

Professor Owen's acceptance of the writings of Lyle on geology or Darwin on biology did not for him discredit the Scriptures. So far as he was concerned, he found nothing in science that was contrary to the Holy Writ. On the contrary, he discovered much to confirm his belief and heighten his faith

[62]

in the Creator of the Universe. "I readily admit," he said, "that Omnipotence could create the world in seven days or in seven seconds." To prove this point he cited Peter and the Psalmist, "One day with the Lord is as a thousand years and a thousand years as one day." Professor Owen regarded Mosaic days as periods of time.

In social matters Professor Owen possessed the enlightened viewpoint of his father. Richard Owen did not envisage a classless society, but like the Danes of a generation later he favored a community in which few should have more than they needed and still fewer have less than they needed. Even before the days of Samuel Gompers, he championed the cause of labor. For it he demanded adequate remuneration to maintain a family in self-respect. He denounced the iron law of wages; he repudiated the principle of *laissez faire*. In a speech delivered before the college chapel in 1874 he declared, "We must do our share for the less favored of our race. We may well foster building associations for the poor, to give them homes, mutual-aid insurance to aid in sickness, hospitals for the sick, asylums for the blind, deaf mutes, idiotic and insane. Nor should we forget the fallen and degraded who by our efforts may perchance be reclaimed." Then, to sustain his argument, he cited examples of social injustice. He supported his brief with Biblical quotations. Long before the constitution had been amended to legalize the graduated income tax, Professor Owen reminded his audiences of the statement from Luke XII, 48, "For unto whomsoever much is given of him shall be much required," and of other equally public-spirited citations.

Professor Owen recognized that as a professor in a state institution he enjoyed a privileged position in society, even though his salary was not bountiful. He possesed security of tenure; the community yielded him generous respect; and he relished the opportunity afforded by his position of gratifying his intellectual interests. There was little more that he desired.

[63]

But he did not overlook *noblesse oblige*. In an address delivered before a meeting of the Odd Fellows, on January 7, 1880, in New Harmony he reminded his listeners that "people should not seek professions for financial gain, but for the service to his fellowmen." The state's objective in maintaining educational institutions was not primarily to enhance the earning power of its graduates, but to advance the community welfare. Each contention he supported with appropriate Biblical quotation.

He was tolerant of all races, for he insisted that they were merely different forms of the same genus. Varying food, climate, habitation, clothing, and proximity to mountains or oceans had caused differences in color. Chemical analysis, he insisted, had revealed no essential difference in the blood of various races. What he had proved as a scientist he supported with Scriptural quotation, from Acts XVII, 24, 26 "God hath made the world,"   "and hath made of one blood all the men that dwell on the face of the earth." Anti-Semites and Ku Kluxers knew better than to appeal to him for aid and comfort.

His tolerant spirit, breadth of sympathy, and enlightened humanitarianism enabled him to see the criminal not only as a culprit but also as a social derelict, the victim of an environment beyond his control: "The wealthy who create the environment are therefore often responsible for the crime." Like modern sociologists he urged prevention of crime and less emphasis upon its punishment. He favored the segregation of juvenile delinquents from the hardened professionals at a time when such advice was not taken for granted.

On economic questions he held utilitarian views, submitting issues to the Benthamite test of the greatest good to the greatest number. Any proposal that satisfied this requirement had Professor Owen's support. In a general sense he subscribed to a *laissez faire* philosophy, and yet his concern for the welfare of the lower classes injected an attitude of benevolent paternalism. The nobility and dignity of humanity in his estimation

[64]

outweighed any claims of wealth or power. Though he endorsed nineteenth-century capitalism, he was conscious of its abuses, for he denounced "gigantic monopolies creating corners and famine, politicians' logrolling and maneuvering."

Though the New Harmony venture had socialistic characteristics, Richard Owen during his professorship did not champion any share-the-wealth program. He insisted that it was "rank injustice to demand that those having property should be compelled to divide with those that have little or none, still worse to enforce this by threat of bloodshed."

While he was interested in the welfare of laborers, he did not want them to coerce capital. Laborers, in his view, while employed were supposed to obey their employers. If they could not peaceably accept the wages offered and the conditions under which they worked, they should resign. His advice was "obey first, remonstrate afterwards."

Though he was essentially kindly by nature, he was an authoritarian. He believed in order and obedience. Citizens should observe the laws of the land, and children should obey their parents "even when they did not comprehend the reason for an order." This affirmation of autocracy did not disturb the harmony of his own household, owing to the judicious exercise of whatever jurisdiction he claimed for himself, and also to his practice of showing good cause for any order. His sons were devoted to their father, and he evinced paternal pride in and affection for them. He extended loans to them without interest charges, and he maintained with them a constant and cordial correspondence. He was helpful to them in practical ways. On his European trip in 1869 he contemplated buying English stock for their herds in New Harmony. Two years later, in 1871, he inspected herds in the neighborhood of Bloomington, Indiana, with a view to their purchase for breeding purposes. He was especially interested in shorthorn cattle, and paid $125 for a fullblooded bull fourteen months old.

In 1872 when his sons contemplated discontinuing farming, he discussed with them their prospective business ventures. He gave them his frank and sympathetic reaction to the establishment of a grocery, a dry goods, or a clothing store in Terre Haute, Indiana. He pointed out that city's population, its number of establishments in the fields in which they were interested, the effect of railroad development in that area of Indiana, and the financial integrity of various economic groups in such a community. "I neglected to mention that Terre Haute has a good Episcopal Church and good graded school," he wrote.

A business matter of more urgent concern in connection with his sons' affairs came to his attention three months later, on May 25, 1872. In going security for friends unworthy of such confidence his sons, Eugene and Horace, had lost considerable money. In response to their letters informing their father of the deception played upon them, Professor Owen wrote, "It is gratifying to find that you both bear up well under your reverses and I hope and believe if you can work through you will acquire thereby business experience and warning which will be of infinite benefit through life. I am sure you will learn sooner than I did not to go security for anyone . . . It is a great satisfaction that amid all your and our trials and troubles, we all keep well and have consciences void of offence, and trust in God to bring us out of our difficulties . . . . No amount that the world contains could induce me to exchange places with those who have been trying to defraud us: in fact have already succeeded to a great extent, because we could not believe the world as bad as it really is." As usual he closed his letter with "warmest love from your mother and myself to each and to all of you, and kisses to our grandchildren, Your affectionate father."

Though he reserved considerable authority for himself as a father, he readily accepted the decrees of his government. He appreciated his adopted country's institutions and was thankful for political freedom: "We have perhaps the fullest and most rational amount of freedom anywhere existing. Compare England with primogeniture and entail, France with her revolution, other nations with imperfect suffrage and censorship of the press . . . with the sober seasoned thought of the American people and you will not hesitate in stating your preference." He traced the development of liberty from ancient Athens to modern America and pledged his faith in its ennobling influence. So long as liberty was not corrupted, he denied any justification for revolution: "It is rebellion to endeavor to enforce by right of arms any supposed injustice when the ballot box is open to us to bring about change if such change is consistent with the will of the majority."

Strangely, this advocate of authority and obedience was also under certain circumstances a patron of revolution. Like Jefferson, or Rousseau, he insisted that "when authority is no longer legally constituted or exercised according to constitutional compact," it is the right and the duty of the people to set aside such an abusive administration.

By 1879 Professor Owen had labored for fifteen years on the Indiana University Campus, and during that time grateful and admiring students had come and gone. Most of them eventually forgot much of what they had learned; but Professor Owen, then sixty-nine years of age, remained in their memory as admirable, judicious, and beloved to them as Colonel Owen had been to the Confederate captives at Camp Morton. His former students have carved no bust in his honor; but through their high regard for him Owen Hall stands as a monument of the esteem in which he was held, not only by his former students but also by his colleagues and other friends.

As he grew older his diaries contain frequent entries about his physical indisposition. The customary teaching load plus the numerous speaking engagements aggravated his physical ailments. Impaired hearing, as a result of a sunstroke, interfered with his teaching and led him to offer his resignation in 1879. In a notable address delivered in the college chapel on May 11, 1879, he took his leave and returned to New Harmony where he spent the remaining eleven years of his life. Indiana University realized the loss it had sustained and, determined to repair it, chose as his successor David Starr Jordan.

Chapter V

PRESIDENT OF PURDUE UNIVERSITY

FOR encouragement to agricultural and technical education the Morrill Act of July, 1862, made available to the several states 30,000 acres for each of their senators and representatives in Congress under the apportionment of 1860. Under its provisions Indiana, with its eleven representatives and two senators, was entitled to 390,000 acres. The Act further stipulated that such land was to be sold and that the proceeds should be invested on terms yielding at least five-per-cent interest. No part of such fund was to be used for the construction of buildings, although ten per cent of the proceeds might be spent for the acquisition of a site for the institution. Indiana, deeply involved in prosecuting the Civil War, did not accept the Federal donation under the Morrill Act until 1865. The proceeds of the sale of that land amounted to $340,000.00.

Interest in the location of the "Indiana Agricultural College," as it was called, was keen. The citizens of Bloomington, Indianapolis, Greenfield, Lafayette, and other cities offered whatever they could to secure it for their respective communities. An offer by John Purdue of $150,000 and one hundred acres of land, provided that the institution was named after him, as well as $50,000 from Tippecanoe County together with land, buildings, and money by the citizens of Battle Ground, was more persuasive than the inducements of other contenders. Another influential consideration in the minds of the Hoosier legislators was anticipated additional bequests from John Purdue, for they hoped that the wealthy benefactor would erect most of the buildings, and that he would be able to enlist even more substantial financial aid from his New York friends. On May 4, 1869, therefore, Tippecanoe County was selected as the future home of Purdue University.

The Board of Trustees, which had been constituted under the provisions of the acceptance of the federal land grant for the establishment of the Indiana Agricultural College, acquired land for the new institution. Ground for the first building was broken on August 8, 1871. Two years later, a residence, a barn, a boarding house, and a dormitory were under construction. The Board of Trustees had also engaged Professor J. S. Hougham to teach mathematics and natural history. From 1872 to 1874 he served in an advisory capacity to the Board.

The selection of a president for the Agricultural College was a matter which should have preceded most of its other actions. In 1872 it tendered an invitation to William S. Clark, then president of the Massachusetts Agricultural College. Though he was offered a salary of $5,000 a year, a large income for that time, he finally declined the invitation. The Board of Trustees was then compelled to find another man, and this time its attention turned to Professor Owen. Obviously he merited consideration. In an era of indifferent academic standards he was a distinguished scholar. In a period of hitherto unparalleled political corruption and financial scandals, his record was without taint. Before the Great Awakening in Indiana, he had urged dynamic intellectualism. He was a man of noble and unostentatious dignity. His whole record was a succession of triumphs, both in academic and administrative responsibilities. He had interested himself in the proposed Agricultural College in 1864 immediately upon assuming his duties at Indiana University. He had drawn up in 1864 a comprehensive plan for the organization of such an institution; he had striven to secure its location at Bloomington, Indiana. His defeat in this matter had not reduced his interest in the College. If the people of Indiana would not bring the Agricultural College to him, why not bring him to it? Mr. Luke A. Burke, a resident of New Harmony and a member of the Board of Trustees from 1871 to 1875, undoubtedly knew Professor Owen personally and could thus vouch for his fitness. The choice of Professor Owen seemed appropriate and wise. On August 13, 1872, he was summoned to Lafayette, Indiana, for an interview during which the Board of Trustees and Professor Owen exchanged their views and at the conclusion of which he was tendered the presidency. He accepted immediately. He was to receive $3,500 a year plus expenses incidental to the office. He then returned to Bloomington and continued his teaching at the opening of the academic year, although it might seem as if his full-time services could have been advantageously employed in organizing the prospective university.

Neither the Board of Trustees nor President Owen took aggressive measures to organize the University during the fall and winter of 1872-73. It was not until May 6, 1873, that the Purdue University Board of Trustees summoned President Owen to Lafayette again, and requested him to draft a plan of organization for the prospective institution. Three and a half months later, on August 26, 1873, he returned to Lafayette and delivered his report on the organization of the University.

This document, which follows, should be viewed in the light of the time in which it was prepared, more than seventy years ago, when tomatoes were suspect and celery was considered a poisonous weed, and oysters a perfect diet for those who had become weary of life. Even twenty years after its composition Elwood Haynes, while driving his first car in Chicago, was ordered off the streets for disorderly conduct. Alexander Graham Bell had not yet patented his telephone, Darwin was viewed as anti-Christ, and Karl Marx was not even taken seriously. Joseph Stalin was still unborn. The customary object of education was to weed out the average and to select the ablest and train them for leadership. That woman of whom the least was heard was held in highest esteem, while Leo Tolstoy regarded woman as the "tool of the devil." The whole philosophy of 1870 was a reflection of the past rather than a forecast of the future. Plastics, zippers, vitamins, and all the paraphernalia of the twentieth century were still many degrees below the dawn of modern America. President Owen's report, though not concerned with atom smashers, relativity, and jet propulsion, was fully abreast of its time.

REPORT TO TRUSTEES OF PURDUE UNIVERSITY
LaFayette, August 26, 1873.

At the last meeting of the Board of Trustees of Purdue University, the undersigned was appointed to prepare a report in accordance with the adoption of the subjoined resolution:

"*Resolved,* That President Owen be requested to prepare a report setting forth what, in his judgment, would be a scheme of education appropriate for the University; as also a scheme for the government and administration of its affairs and property, and that he report the same to the Board at its next meeting, together with his suggestions in reference to the selection of a Faculty and such other employes as may be required for the operation of the various administrative and economical interests of the University; keeping in view the laws of Congress in relation to Agricultural Colleges."

In accordance with the above resolution the undersigned submits the following

REPORT:
I. THE PLAN OF EDUCATION.

No plan or scheme of education would in the opinion of your committee be complete, which failed to take into account the necessity of developing the physical and moral faculties, as well as the intellectual, to which latter frequently almost exclusive attention is paid. For the purpose of having the young man, at the close of his college career, sound in body and morals and well advanced in intellectual acquirements, your committee would recommend for the three departments, respectively, a system of which the following may give an outline perhaps sufficiently in detail for the purpose of discussion and decision:

[72]

1. *Physical Training and Development.*—For this purpose, every student, physically capable, should be required to take military drill at least two days in the week for two hours in the afternoon. The other days in the week, every student should labor either on the farm, in the garden, stable or work-shop, or if ladies are admitted, then in the kitchen, laundry, &c., at least two hours each weekday afternoon, Saturdays excepted, which might be devoted to excursions with professors, either geologizing, botanizing, &c., or visiting large manufacturing establishments. If funds permit, there should, by all means, be a large building, the lower part of which should be used as a gymnasium and drill ground, especially in wet weather.

Facility should be afforded for others, who desire to labor more, to be employed at a fair remuneration, as long as they choose, provided, this does not prevent their always being prepared with the requisite recitations. There should also be grounds suitable for sports and recreative amusements; also for bathing, and in summer, swimming, at safe places, under proper supervision. If immediate arrangements for baths can not be made, there should be means of access, at all times, to abundance of cold and hot water for the purpose of a tepid sponge bath when the weather is cold.

2. *Moral Instruction.*—To render the preservation of a good moral tone practicable it is recommended that all students, on entering, should present testimonials regarding their conduct while at other educational institutions of preparatory character; also that a lecture should be given every Saturday morning by one of the professors, the discourse having a bearing upon the formation of character, laws of life and health, or some subject tending to elevate the moral tone and standard of public sentiment in the Institution. Each professor should also lecture on a religious or moral subject, in rotation, on Sunday afternoons, and students should be admonished to attend church and Sunday-school, and be required to be present at morning prayer in chapel.

It is recommended further, that the whole number attending college classes be arrayed in sections of from ten to fifteen members, each section being placed under the supervision of a student of the senior class, who shall assemble them twice a week in order to afford opportunity for discussing any matters of complaint, dispute or difficulty involving the members of that section, each senior thus in charge to be, to some extent, responsible for their good conduct. On Saturday the united sections shall meet in general assembly under the supervision of the President of the College, and through their section-chiefs report such cases as require further adjudication.

When cases requiring apparently serious discipline arise, if the student accused request a trial by jury, the Secretary of the Faculty shall, through the Janitor, select in alphabetical order from the roster of seniors and juniors, three of the former and four of the latter, designating one as foreman. These, after hearing the case, in the presence of the President as presiding officer, and of the Secretary (questions being handed in writing by any of the jurors to be put to the principal or witnesses by the President), shall decide, by a majority vote, on his guilt or innocence, and, if guilty, recommend the penalty; and the Faculty, on hearing a statement of the case from the Secretary, who shall keep record of the same, shall approve or disapprove said penalty, by a majority vote, affixing another if disapproved.

This plan has been tried in England and on the Continent of Europe with success; the experience being that students are usually, if any thing, more severe than the Faculty.

Students, especially in the earlier years of the college, before a strong, moral, public opinion is known permanently to pervade the community, should promptly be invited to leave, if their influence is injurious. Yet, if they demand a trial on the general charge, they should be allowed one.

3. *Intellectual Advancement.*—The course of instruction should, in the judgment of your committee, be such that, when the student ends his four years' course, he should be capable of taking charge, practically, as agent, director or assistant director, and the like, in any department for which he has been specially qualifying himself, such as teaching analysis in a laboratory, or directing a manufacturing laboratory, superintending hands in a mine, or in iron works, (furnaces, bloomeries, rolling-mills, nail factories) surveying land in the capacity of land surveyor, or railroads, turnpikes, &c., as civil engineer, able to direct dyeing, say in a woolen factory, to become assistant engineer in charge of a locomotive or for a stationary engine, to superintend a large farm, or market garden, or plantation, as overseer, or to take charge of a large stable, herd of cattle, flock of sheep, pens of hogs, with a knowledge of the habits,

wants, diseases and remedies among those domestic animals, or to undertake as contractor or overseer to supervise the hands constructing some earthworks, embankments, &c.

To this end, it seems desirable that, while there is a four years' course, embracing certain studies with which all should be familiar, there might be a corresponding series of equivalent studies, mathematical, chemical, geological and the like permitted; the specialty to take the lead. For those not desiring to graduate, there might be a yet more special course permitted, and to those desiring some languages there might be facilities for the optional course of Latin during the freshman and sophomore years, and one of Greek, during the junior year; or two years of a modern language, after the necessary preparation in the grammars of these languages, during the preparatory year.

In order to meet the requirements of Congress, as also to satisfy the expectations and demands of our citizens, it is earnestly recommended that, if practicable, as much of the course as possible should be entered upon about the 1st of April next, the necessary steps being taken previously to advertise the University and invite students, as well as to determine such items connected therewith, such as the terms of entrance, course of study, &c., as may best suffice for preliminary work; also to obtain from the most reliable sources and at the most truly economical rates all that is absolutely necessary in connection with the tuition of students, and boarding and lodging of students, professors, employes, &c., for the carrying on of such preliminary work; it being made the special duty of some one to negotiate all the matters to the best advantage.

II. RECOMMENDATIONS FOR FACULTY AND EMPLOYES.

In this regard, it may be well first to examine what it seems desirable and in fact absolutely necessary to have ultimately, if we would maintain a high position among colleges, and secondly, how near we can come to that ideal, with our present available means.

It is scarcely possible for a college to carry on the necessary chairs, filled with able men, and meet the current demands of a museum, library, and keep up the chemical and philosophical apparatus, even after these have been well organized, with a less fund than $32,000 to $36,500 per annum, as required for the following purposes:

[75]

Insurance, probably over this amount, but say_____ $1,000 00
Library, Museum, Laboratory and Philosophical apparatus__ 1,500 00
Eight full professorships, $2,000, (viz.: 1. Moral and Mental
    Science. 2. Chemistry. 3. Physics. 4. Mathematics.
    5. Geology, etc. 6. Natural History. 7. English Lit'
    erature. 8. Languages_____ 16,000 00
Salary of President_____ 3,500 00
Military Professor, $1,000; Taxidermist, $1,000; Mathemati-
    cal assistant, $1,000_____ 3,000 00
Principal of Preparatory Department, $1,000; Music
    Teacher, $1,000; Janitor, $600_____ 2,600.00
Farm Superintendent, $1,500; Accountant, who is also
    House Superintendent, $1,500_____ 3,000 00
Incidental expense for fuel, lights, repairs, &c._____ 1,000 00
Traveling expenses, etc., connected with keeping up with
    times _____ 400 00
Advertising, stationery, postage, printing &c._____ 500 00

    At the lowest estimates therefore_____[sic] $32,000 00
    To the above ought really to be added:
A Veterinary Surgeon, teacher of Human and Comparative
    Anatomy _____ $2,000 00
A teacher of Modern Languages, say_____ 1,500 00
And (as in the Kansas Agricultural College) foreman of
    Mechanical Department_____ 1,000 00

                                                           $4,500 00

    Total _____[sic] $36,500 00
As however for the present we have not the above amount,
and yet desire to open April next, we could meantime do with
$21,000, to be expended somewhat in the following manner:
For insurance_____ $1,000 00
For Museum, Library, Chemical and Philosophical apparatus 400 00
For incidental expenses, for fuel, lights, &c._____ 400 00
For advertising, postage, stationery, printing, &c._____ 400 00
For traveling expenses and similar incidentals_____ 300 00
For President's salary_____ 3,500 00
For five full Professorships, $2,000, (viz: 1. Chemistry.
    2. Natural Philosophy. 3. Mathematics. 4. Natural
    History. 5. English Literature_____[sic] 2,000 00
For Taxidermist, $1,000; Military Professor, $500; Primary
    Preparatory Department, $1,000_____[sic] 2,000 00
For Janitor, $500; Book-keeper, $500_____ 1,000 00
For Farm Superintendent, (besides a house and use of cow
    and horse)_____ 1,500 00

    Total at a very low college estimate_____[sic] $21,000 00

The next question is how to meet this expenditure. The answer is by allowing some margin in the boarding and by charging a matriculation and graduation fee, the former of $5, the latter of $10, also a Janitor's fee of $3 per term (or $9 per annum) but no tuition fee. The income would then stand about thus, when we have been able to secure two hundred students:

Interest on Scrip, &c., about	$17,500 00
Matriculation fee of two hundred students, $5	1,000 00
Graduation fee of ten Seniors $10	100 00
Janitor's fee from two hundred students, $9	1,800 00
Leaving to be made up by profit on board, at least	600 00
Total income	$21,000 00

It is earnestly recommended to fulfill the requirements of Congress, by commencing on this scale by the 1st of April next. To that end it would be advisable, in order to be in a state of readiness, to take the following preliminary steps, some assistant details regarding which are given under the next head, that of administration.

1.   To elect at this meeting four additional Professors, one Taxidermist, one Principal Preparatory Department, one Janitor, one House Superintendent (to be paid $800 or $1,000 out of boarding house fund, increased by $500 as above for book-keeper, if he keep also all the accounts), also one Superintendent of Farm. These two latter would probably have to be on the premises all the year, hence $1,500 each seems low enough. None of these salaries to begin until the 1st of April, or such time as their services are needed.

2.   It must be made the duty of some one to purchase, after careful selection in the best market, the necessary furniture for Dormitory and Boarding-house, as well as for Chapel and Class-rooms, the necessary kitchen apparatus, Dining-room and chamber ware, bed and table linen, blankets, comforts and toweling.

3.   To make the inquiries and contracts regarding staple articles of provisions, so that at the shortest notice these can be on the ground by the 1st of April; permanent supplies of such vegetables and fruits as will keep, being laid in before that time.

[77]

III. ADMINISTRATION.

It is recommended that each department be self-sustaining, so far as practicable, and that accurately kept accounts should show the financial condition of each.

The different departments might be subdivided thus:

1. Educational Department, under the Faculty.

2. Agricultural Department, under management of Farm Superintendent, with the necessary hands, students, &c.

3. Horticultural Department, under management of Professor of Botany, Head Gardener, and students.

4. A Boarding-house, to be superintended by a House Superintendent, Steward, and the necessary number of waiters.

5. A Laundry, under direction of a matron and head laundress, with necessary assistants.

6. A Lodging House or Dormitory, under charge of the House Superintendent, for male students; a separate building if ladies are admitted, to be under charge of the matron.

7. The Department of Accounts, to be under the management of the Accountant (who may, if thought best, be also House Superintendent). All accounts to be collected weekly, and all payments to be made to hands (viz: work-hands), &c., weekly, either by heads of Departments or House Superintendent. Accounts to be kept by him deduced from the blotter of each head of the Department, showing at intervals of six months (or for Farm and Garden of twelve months), the state of accounts. To all departments the cooperative aid of the President should be given.

A thorough system of drainage should be entered into, after survey made, and carried out, under supervision of Mathematical Department, aided by students.

A thorough system of fire organization to be adopted, by having the necessary lightning rods under supervision of Professor of Natural Philosophy; also means of communicating along each roof in case of fire in stairway, ladders and hooks, axes and pick-axes, to be always in readiness; also a roster of night watchers, either hired or taken from among older reliable students, who should be paid for such services.

A complete system of ventilation should be provided for, so that, if means have not sufficiently been adopted in the original construction of any building, panes of glass, and panels of doors having no transoms, should be made movable. As being safer from accidental fire and wholesomer than stoves, open grates, burning coal and having a blower to help kindle the fire, when out or low, are strongly recommended; next to those, sheet-iron air-tight stoves would perhaps be least liable to the inconvenience of decomposing the air, and, with thorough ventilation, might not heat the head, while the feet remain cold, as is the case in many stove-rooms.

A dietary should be adopted which should at the same time give sufficient variety from day to day, and be of not the most expensive kind, yet nutritious, palatable and wholesome, avoiding the free use of pork, meats fried in grease, rich pastry and the like, as being highly injurious to those having more work of the brain than of the muscles.

It is further recommended to give animal food only once a day, and to use largely of corn meal and unbolted flour for bread and mush, in order to avoid the great evils incident on a sedentary life, constipation and hemorrhoids. It is also recommended that to all who will abstain from tea and coffee a somewhat reduced rate of weekly board should be given, also that various farinaceous puddings and the like be substituted most of the time for the rich pastry too commonly used as dessert. For the sake of health, the meals, if three are taken each day, should be at least six hours apart, and served with great punctuality at the appointed hour.

As the annual funds at present available from Congressional grant are not even sufficient for such a corps of Professors as would give undoubted pre-eminence to the institution, it is recommended (besides using every available means for securing the proceeds of the public lands at the next meeting of Congress) to place the price of board and lodging at such a rate, not to exceed, however, $4.00 per week, as shall leave some margin of profit, in order to meet the current expenses of the College, besides a janitor's fee, &c., as already suggested. The matriculation fee would prevent, or at least check, persons from giving all the trouble to arrange classes, &c., and then in two or three weeks, taking their departure, if homesick or dissatisfied; or if they went, would reimburse for the trouble.

To insure regularity and uniformity regarding seats, clothing, &c., the use of numbers might be adopted, giving one to each

student, when he or she entered (if ladies are admitted) reserv-
ing the numbers made vacant by departures, for the next comers,
thus readily having a mark by which to designate places at the
table and avoid confusion or loss by having this number on
clothing, napkin rings and other property. This need not prevent their changing places at the table at intervals by drawing
tickets, so as to prevent cliques or dissatisfaction, if one place
is deemed better than another.

It is strongly recommended to cook by steam, either by con-
necting with a boiler if there be one, or by using the Eagle
Steamer, carrying usually seven pounds, and made by E. E. Sill,
of Rochester, New York; also for baking meats, bread, &c., an
apparatus made by J. S. Blodget, of Burlington, Vermont, size
No. 8, which will bake for one hundred and fifty; the other
cooking to be done at a large range of most approved form,
with cast iron plates on top, central fire, side ovens, &c., such
as made by Messrs. L. F. Duparquet & Huot, 24 and 26,
Wooster Street, New York City. There should be a hood
overhead to carry off all the effluvia, and if necessary that a
stove should be used, one weighing about one hundred and
fifty pounds, called William Doyle's Great American cooking
stove, made at Albany, New York, will be found excellent. By
running two straps of iron, let into the floor from the kitchen
to the dining room, for the passage of a dumb waiter, on four
cast iron wheels with two outside shelves and one central higher
shelf for carrying the vessels and dishes of cooked vegetables,
fruit, &c., much labor is saved. For ordinary purposes French's
hall stove, from Buffalo, capable of receiving a four foot stick
of wood, will be found efficient. For water, instead of expensive
wells, in order to use soft water, which is more conducive to
health and comfort than hard, it is earnestly advised to construct
numerous outside cement cisterns, perhaps eight or ten feet in
depth; then, inside one or more of the large buildings, to sink
a well or cement cistern not so far as to reach water, into which
the water from these cisterns can be run through laminated
asphaltum pipes, such as are made in Rochester, New York, the
water cleared and purified by passing through a gravel and
charcoal filter before it reaches the well; thence it can be pumped
either as wanted, or sent by machinery, to a large reservoir
above, from which any part of the premises can be supplied by
simply turning a stop-cock.

For flour it might be profitable to have one of Lane Bros.' Iron Mills, made in Milbrook, Dutchess County, New York, and to purchase dried fruit and desiccated vegetables from the Alden Company or from the Shakers Society at Sonyea, New York, who are careful to dry all of one kind together, thus insuring uniformity in cooking sufficiently.

If earth closets are used instead of water closets, Goux' plan is said to be the best, and the most effective disinfectants, besides earth, are carbolate of lime, copperas and the like; a cheap yet efficient substitute, being free use of lime and plaster.

For sewerage the round tile pipe may be laid, the main sewer requiring a pipe from four to six inches in diameter.

In supplying wood or coal to students, it is recommended to make this a special charge above the use of room and of board, either measuring to them in cord and half cord stacks a given amount, and letting them cut, saw, split, carry, &c., or in case ladies are admitted, employing a man with a leather apron slung over his shoulder and having a handle of leather on the lower side to carry from the horse or steam sawing machine to the boxes in the rooms, which boxes have all been made to hold a definite quantity of wood of ordinary size for the fire-place or stove of that room. The coal in the same way can be carried in iron buckets or scuttles, holding a given weight, which amount, when the box is full, can be given in at the office and charged for that week in settlement of students' accounts. The expense of lights being small, it is thought best, unless gas is used, to supply to each student a lamp and a half gallon coal oil can, and either let them purchase in town or supply them from the office, charging cost for the same. They might also furnish their own blacking and brushes.

To secure the above purchases most advantageously some one might be designated by the Trustees a sufficient time before the opening of College to visit personally or correspond with parties offering favorable terms at large establishments. Should a supply of excellent unbolted flour not be obtained near, it can be had in Danville, New York, at $8.00 per barrel, freight usually $1.35 per barrel; and oat meal can be had from Messrs. Johnson & Co. (formerly from Canada), now at Rockford, Illinois.

As a means of meeting a want, which is sure to be felt by professors, whether with or without families, also, however,

[81]

for the sake of economy when engaging officials, assistants, &c., by giving board and thus reducing salary; but more especially for the purpose of incorporating the students' inner life and sympathies with those of the professors, the following plan with regard to lodging and boarding is recommended. The College grounds being one and a half miles from the city center, provision should be made for the accommodation of professors, and head employes. If a building were erected at the cost say of $15,000 (by borrowing the money, if necessary at 10 per cent. interest, or by forming a joint stock company and selling out when any wish to remove) this cost to include the necessary furniture, and the house to contain say eighteen rooms, then each professor could take from two to three rooms, according to the size of his family, and pay an average of $2 per week or $100 per annum for each furnished room. This would bring in yearly $1,800, of which $1,500 would pay 10 per cent. interest on cost, $300 be left for wear and tear of furniture. If this building were erected near the boarding-house, those who choose could eat at the same time and place with the students, showing an example of obedience to the laws of health in diet and of courteous manners, thereby, without special display of authority, &c., insensibly preserving order and good feeling.

If this plan is approved and the building not large enough for all, it might be enlarged and cost even less per room for erection, or two buildings could be erected on the same plan. Possibly some of the building associations might furnish the means. And if the plan of eating with the students does not seem the best, a kitchen and appurtenances, as well as dining-room and library and reading-room, might be held in common and a steward be found to furnish board of good quality at a fixed rate per week. Either plan would give professors and their families more time to devote to the interests of the institution.

Nothing has been said about the ways and means for raising the funds necessary to meet the purchases for furniture, kitchen and dining-room requisites and the like, digging the wells, constructing cisterns, out-houses, &c., none of which can be dispensed with, to say nothing of the Library, Museum, Chemical and Philosophical apparatus, class-room and chapel furniture, barn, stable, conservatory, &c., &c., but it is anticipated that such expenditures could be met by part of the Purdue fund or the County subscription, or that additional aid must be had from the State, if Congress fails to give us the additional proceeds of lands.

As abundance of good pure water is essential to health, comfort and safety from fire, it is urged that ample tanks, wells, &c., be provided. If a small steam engine is employed to obtain the necessary power, this power might at intervals, as already suggested, pump water into a tank or reservoir, high enough to distribute water over the buildings.

Until there shall be a main building adequate for chapel and recitation rooms, it is suggested, if rooms in the dormitory would be insufficient, to commence at once a cheap building of considerable dimensions, the lower story all in one, to serve meantime as chapel and room for public exercises, the upper story to consist of moderate sized rooms suitable for temporary class rooms. When no longer needed for these purposes, the lower story might be used as a gymnasium, for exercises in inclement weather, and the upper rooms, as cheap dormitories for employes, help, &c. Or if preferred and no other means have been provided, the whole building could be fitted up for a Museum.

As regards the fitting up of a Museum, it is earnestly recommended that the plan and specification should be made out by Professor Ward, of Rochester, who has had long experience in this department. He would charge $50 for the same, and would put in sealed proposals with the others when bids are called for. With reference to filling the Museum, or rather meeting its first wants for illustrative materials, the undersigned is willing, if the freight is paid on his collection of books, about 1,200 volumes, as also on his fossils and minerals, zoological specimens and charts, to have most of the books placed in the library to be loaned to the students during his connection with the institution, and to have all his collection, which would be ample for present class illustration, used in College, either by his receiving a fair rental for their use or such compensation by purchase as would be affixed by disinterested judges on the specimens, as well as on some books, such as the American Journal of Science, since about 1830, New York Natural History reports, &c., &c. The zoological cabinet could be made up to a great extent, especially in Mammalogy and Ornithology, by specimens shot and prepared, either as skeletons, or stuffed, or

[83]

both (and particularly the comparative anatomy of our domestic animals be thus exhibited) by the labor of Dr. Lemon as Taxidermist and Curator, also of W. Neil, should these persons be selected for the positions to which they are recommended, especially if Professor E. E. Henry should be engaged and contribute his labors.

Correspondence should also be had with various societies and public institutions, such as the Smithsonian, and with liberal individuals, asking exchanges, donations, &c., &c.

As an additional means of health, the best and most recent information should be obtained regarding water or earth closets, and such plan be adopted as would best subserve the purpose of health, convenience, neatness, &c.; all buildings calculated to detract from the pleasant aspect and surroundings of a beautiful home, being sheltered from view by hedges of osage, privet, arbor vitae, and the like. As far as practicable, extensive gravel walks through campus, garden, &c., should afford dry walking, even after rains, and plats in all directions, with shrubbery and flowers chiefly perennial, should enliven the students' home, so that homesickness would be unheard of, especially when to these attractive surroundings would be added the sympathizing kindness, which professors, employes, older students, in fact all, should be urged to extend to new comers, until they felt themselves indeed at home, and until they could realize the fact that their student life readily could be one of attractiveness, happiness and preparation for a future of usefulness to themselves and others, and was calculated to prepare them to fulfill the commands and responsibilities assigned them by their Divine Creator.

Respectfully submitted,
RICHARD OWEN.

There is no statement of the Board of Trustees' reaction to the Report, but an anonymous critic writing under the signature of "Humbug" contributed a slashing article in the *Indiana Farmer,* which was reprinted in the December 24, 1873, issue of the *Lafayette Journal,* in which he attacked President Owen's Report. He found not one item that he could endorse. "When I read this report of the President—which is as good as law—I must say I was much disappointed—not to say disgusted." . . . "There is a four year's course; the plan is that of 'physical training and development'. For this purpose every student should be required to take a military drill at least two days a week, for two hours in the afternoon, besides farm and shop work every other day in the week; and two hours each day, Saturday excepted, to be devoted to geological and botanical exercises. In the name of my grandfather's horn plow handles, what need of military drill, when there is plenty of peaceful farm work to healthfully develop every muscle in the body?" The critic objected to the instruction in morals and chapel attendance, and to jury trial of students; because President Owen averred that this system had worked well in England and on the continent of Europe, the anonymous critic burst out, "May the continent perish with dry rot and England be affected with 'holler-horn'. If they are to be punished they want it measured out by the faculty or the trustees." He ridiculed President Owen's hope that a graduate of Purdue would be competent to become assistant director or director of a factory or supervisor of a farm or of a large cattle barn. He declared such courses as chemistry, physics, mathematics, English literature and language to be unnecessary: "Now by all the teeth of a Norwegian harrow, I cannot see in this list, where a young man could be fitted for taking charge of anything . . ." He recommended practical experience under men who did not confuse practice with theory. He poured heaps of scorn on that section of the Report which concerned diet for the students and the recommendations for heating and ventilating. And as for the salary of $2,000 a year for the faculty members, that was altogether too little.

To this verbal musketade President Owen felt constrained to defend himself. On January 1, 1874, in the *Lafayette Journal* he declared that the Report had not been written for general distribution but had been intended largely as a basis of con-

[85]

fidential discussion with the Board of Trustees. After an exchange of views he supposed that certain parts of the Report might be deleted, while he also anticipated that suggestions of the Board might be added. In all circumstances he aimed to carry out policies on which he and the Board would agree. To the criticism that he had proposed two hours of military drill each week President Owen reminded the critic that the state of Indiana was under obligation to the general government to offer military drill as a part of its curriculum, and that he had prescribed the minimum accepted under the Morrill Act. President Owen also defended his recommendation of sheet iron stoves in preference to cast iron heaters on the ground that the latter, according to the testimony of chemists, generated carbonic oxide, which sheet iron stoves did not. He defended his dietary recommendations by his knowledge of physiological functions learned from years of teaching of physiology and studies while acquiring his degree of doctor of medicine at Nashville Medical College. In defense of his program of moral instruction he insisted that he believed "moral development more important than the intellectual."

"Why the critic should object to being tried by his peers (as our jury system) I am wholly at a loss to understand," he wrote "if he had said it does not work in practice, I could have seen some force in his objection, but it is certainly a system for republicans rather than for monarchists. If the Trustees disapprove of that or any other recommendation, they have only to say so and I acquiesce cheerfully.

"To the charge of nepotism I offer nothing but facts, and leave the judgment to an enlightened public. My older son, who had farmed over ten years, and is one of the best judges of cattle and hogs, had offered his services for farm superintendent long before I had the slightest idea of offering myself for the presidency. He had testimonials from ex-Governor Baker, Professor Cox and Major Palmer. My younger son,

being conversant with general business, I spoke of him as probably suitable for House Superintendent, but at the same time
gave the name of another gentleman for the same position.
My son had advised against my presenting his name, and as
soon as he learned it was objectionable withdrew it. . . . I
admit it was an error on my part to present my younger son's
name because of the *appearance* of endeavoring to bring in
my whole family, as they are all that I have."

And finally to refute the charge of incompetence for the
presidency he cited his experience of operating a mill for seven
years, a farm for ten years, his service in the Mexican War
as a captain, his period in the Civil War as a colonel, and his
twenty years of connection with educational institutions. During that period of forty-six years he challenged any one to
discover an abuse of public or private trust or any dereliction
of public duty. "If forty-six years of an honorable course is
not sufficient to establish a man's character," he asked, "what
term of years is required?"

He concluded by saying that the public had a perfect right
to examine closely all the details regarding the Agricultural
College, in order to criticize and make recommendations for
its success, which would be difficult enough of attainment
with all kind aid which friends might give. But, he continued,
it was a different matter when persons, who were uninformed
on most of the points, undertook to abuse those who were
striving disinterestedly for the welfare of the people.

President Owen's rejoinder was not directed so much against
the anonymous critic as it was against the editor of the *Lafayette
Journal* for having given space to it in his columns and thereby,
Owen believed, countenanced the criticisms.

The report made little provision for engineering education
as such. The paucity on this point is explained on the ground
that the engineering profession had not yet been specialized.
The chemical industry had not yet attained any significance,

and the dynamo had not even been invented; hence the omission of courses in chemical and electrical engineering. Natural philosophy and mechanics offered whatever information was then required in mechanical engineering, while surveying and allied courses were to be given under mathematics.

No sooner was one critic silenced than another one raised his voice. The editor of the *Educationist,* Mr. A. C. Shortridge, who succeeded Owen in the Purdue presidency, wrote in his January, 1874, issue that the selection of President Owen was a "mistake" and insisted that "his immediate resignation is a necessity." With a tone of lofty concern for the public interest, and of regret to say anything that might wound the sensibilities of any of his readers, he insisted that the editor of an educational journal of the state had some responsibilities for sound education. Without mentioning a single disqualification of President Owen, he proceeded to enumerate the qualities which the president of the institution ought to possess. His spirit should direct and inspire the work of each department: "He should be a man of broad views, liberal culture, practical common sense, and having the power to generalize and to organize." To secure such a man the Board of Trustees should not hesitate to pay $10,000 a year if necessary, for "one ten-thousand-dollar a year man was better than ten one-thousand-dollar a year men in any position where an unlimited amount of brain power is needed." As to the curriculum and purpose of the University the writer had definite ideas too: "It is the theory and practice of mechanism and farming that should and will command the attention of the student, if this school is to be different from other schools."

An editorial in the *Indiana School Journal* of January, 1874, contended that Dr. Owen's scholarship "no one doubts, and his ability to organize and control are yet to be tested." Criticism of the purposes of the University poured in from other influential sources and additional doubt was cast upon President

Owen's ability to organize the institution. Praise was heaped upon his scientific and cultural accomplishments in order to infer his impracticality as an administrator. Criticism of this nature did not endear the new position to President Owen.

There were other reasons why Professor Owen lacked enthusiasm for the presidency. He and the Board of Trustees differed on essential policies. He insisted upon greater emphasis on instruction in agriculture than the Board had in mind. Furthermore, he wanted better dormitories than those designed by the Board. As a man trained in medicine and devoted to scholarship, he was conscious of the injury to the body from prolonged mental exertion in quarters lacking in human comfort. There was always something of an artist in the Owens, and Richard has been called the most typical of the family. Though a scientist, he also had artistic appreciation and he had a vision of Purdue University nestling in a forest of shade trees. Mr. Martin Peirce, a member of the Board, envisioned the Campus along lines of his own, and they did not harmonize with Professor Owen's. The members of the Board announced that the students were there to learn, and supposedly not to saunter in sylvan beauty. Thus disagreements accumulated, and as they did Professor Owen appreciated more than ever the tranquility of an academic career. Not only that. The Board of Trustees of Indiana University also appreciated him, and it was much loath to lose him. To assure his continuance on that campus it offered him the curatorship of the new museum there. This would enable Professor Owen to do that which appealed to him most of all, teaching and research.

The presidency of Purdue University would have compelled him to concern himself with such matters as the selection of a dozen faculty members, arrangement of classrooms, dormitory facilities, purchase of food for the students, extraction of appropriations from the legislature, and the continuous adjustment of differences among prima donna temperaments. Pro-

[89]

fessor Owen preferred wrestling with involved ideas to struggling with complicated situations. His vocation was his hobby;
his pursuit and his pastime were identical: the conquest of
the unknown. Administrative work to him was not as engaging as the romance of the intellectual chase. As president
his activity would have been confined largely to the campus.
As professor he could, and did, regard himself as the center
of the universe, and it was his playground.

Until the outburst of criticism President Owen had not im-
mersed himself in the problems of organizing Purdue University.
He, who confided to his Diary systematically week by week
for years the number of socks, handkerchiefs, shirts and under-
wear that he sent to the laundry, was strangely silent about
his new responsibility. In these intimate volumes he recorded
weddings and funerals which he solemnized, articles which he
published and taxes which he paid, but scarcely a word about
his new position. He made but four trips to Lafayette, Indiana, and on the last of these, after his resignation, he sold
his collection of minerals and fossils to the institution.[1] He
never was in residence, and he never drew a salary.

Though President Owen and the Board of Trustees failed
to see eye to eye on questions of fundamental importance, he

---

[1] Reimbursements on account of expenses incurred in connection
with Professor Owen's presidency of Purdue, and occasions on which
he was in Lafayette in connection with the organization of Purdue
University.

August 13, 1872	Interviewed by the Board of Trustees, and accepted presidency.	
May 7, 1873	Two days in meeting with Board of Trustees plus four days in transit_____$	39.00
August 26, 1873	One day in meeting with Board of Trustees plus four days traveling_____	36.00
August 26, 1874	Receipt for fossils and minerals_____	675.00
	Receipt for books_____	180.00
	Expense while arranging and labeling fossils and minerals _____	46.60
		$976.60

did not allow rancor to mar his feeling. On March 1, 1874, he offered his resignation in a dignified letter in which he expressed the hope that some one would be found "who will more fully carry out your views. Allow me to wish for the Institution a successful Future." Thus closed the incident, and Professor Owen continued his teaching at Indiana University with little change, if any, in his life.

It is perhaps unprofitable to speculate on Professor Owen's success had he continued as President of Purdue University. Yet it is difficult to omit part of a letter of March 21, 1941, on this matter from Dr. William Lowe Bryan, President-emeritus of Indiana University, to Dr. Edward C. Elliott, President of Purdue University. Dr. Byran declared that until he had read the account by Hattie Lou Winslow and Joseph R. H. Moore of "Camp Morton under Richard Owen" in *Camp Morton 1861-1865* in the Indiana Historical Society Publications he "had no idea that he was an executive of masterly ability as he proved himself to be at Camp Morton. It was certainly an ill day for Purdue when this great man and great executive was set aside. . . ."

Chapter VI

RETIREMENT

ON his ninetieth birthday, March 8, 1931, Justice Oliver Wendell Holmes was presented with a collection of essays written by his friends. In response to this mark of affection the gallant and colorful old veteran of the bench said, "In this symposium my part is only to sit in silence. To express one's feeling as the end draws near is too intimate a task. But I may mention one thought that comes to me as a listener-in. The riders in a race do not stop short when they reach the goal. There is a little finishing canter before coming to a standstill. There is time to hear the kind voices of friends and to say to oneself, 'The work is done.' But just as one says that, the answer comes: 'The race is over but the work is never done while the power to work remains.' "

Professor Owen, like Justice Holmes, continued to canter after the race. He shifted his pace from an intellectual gallop to a mental trot with browsings hither and yon along the course.

Release from teaching left more time for reading, research, and writing, with a consequent acceleration in articles published. Many of these were in the field of physics and were concerned primarily with magnetism and the molecular theory. In the issue of the *American Meteorological Journal* for January 1, 1890, he published a notable article on the construction and behavior of magnets. Simultaneously he was conducting experiments with resin and discovered that a filament of resin suspended free from effects of torsion assumed a paramagnetic

position. He secured compass leaves from Minnesota and suspended them by the petiole, and they likewise assumed a paramagnetic direction. To prove that all plants did not possess
this quality, he experimented with blades of grass, as well as
with beach leaves, and observed that these were neutral. He
extended his experiments to prove that not all leaves of the
compass-plant face uniformly north and south as was claimed
by Professor Asa Gray in his manual. He discovered that
the lower leaves faced east and west, but that the upper leaves
had magnetic qualities which impelled them to face north and
south. On these and other subjects he exchanged a voluminous
correspondence with men of similar interests. He observed
that sound traveled about thirteen miles a minute in air, but
that in water it traveled about four times as fast as in air,
while in iron it traveled almost three times as fast as it did
in water. He purchased the latest books in his field as they
came off the press. He spent sixty-eight dollars for a globe
and considerable sums for other equipment used in his scientific pursuit.

Weather is a topic of universal interest. Most people, however, limit their reactions to sweeping and inexact generalizations. On this subject, as in so many others, Professor Owen
could not divest himself of his usual scientific approach. He recorded the thermal and barometric readings day by day. He
observed and recorded the temperature readings in the sun
and in the shade at various times of the day. He took thermal
readings at six, twelve, twenty-four, and forty-eight inches below the surface of the ground when the temperature was
135 degrees Fahrenheit in the sun. He took temperature readings in wells varying from twenty-four to thirty feet in depth
during the summer months, and he discovered that during very
hot days the temperature rose slightly but that it varied very
little with the seasons. In summer he usually found that
the thermal readings were about fifty-eight degrees Fahrenheit,

while in winter they dropped to only fifty-six degrees. He also noted that in these wells the water rose and fell with the level of the Wabash River although it was almost half a mile distant

Geology continued to monopolize a major share of his reading. "Earthquakes," he said, "possess for me a peculiar interest from their intimate connection with geological structure of the world." Among many other volumes which he read was Volume II of Darwin's *On the Origin of Species*. He believed that seismic forces moved along an important Great Circle from Panama to the neighborhood of the Gulf of Ueracybo and thence with the Great Circle, which forms the eastern shore of Asia, then swerved across the Pacific to the vicinity of Caracas and then north to Indiana and Illinois. He possessed a seismograph of his own and detected disturbances that lasted from six to eight seconds. He noted the number of earthquakes per year in the various parts of the world and tried to account for the frequency and character of these disturbances. Tashkent experienced five earthquakes a year, he observed; Lake Baikal was probably a volcanic fissure or chasm. His seismic researches were designed to reach at least suggestive results as to the probable causes, immediate and remote, of the many changes through which our planet has passed or is now passing. His researches dealt primarily with the earlier refrigeration, as well as with the later seismic period, of the geological formation.

He was perhaps one of the earlist geopoliticians, for he agreed with Huxley that geography should be viewed "not as a new chronicle of regions and battles but as a chapter in the development of the race and history of civilization." Certainly he more clearly perceived the significance of geography as a factor in history than most scholars did.

He believed that maps should be not merely a drawing of the countries' outlines, but physical miniatures of the countries themselves, showing as many of their geographical characteristics as possible. He constructed in his study and workshop, with the aid of an assistant, many of these maps of every continent and of many countries. These revealed the depressions of rivers and river valleys, the elevations of mountains, and the flat surfaces of plains and prairies. In 1889 he entered an international contest sponsored by the king of the Belgians "for the best system of popularizing geography." Of the sixty competitors Professor Owen was one of four to receive honorable mention, the prize being awarded to a German professor. Professor Owen submitted an essay in which he advocated the use of relief maps to illustrate the natural geography of countries, and sent to Brussels numerous specimens modelled in putty as illustrations.

Professor Owen also contributed a paper to the Bologna session of the International Congress of Geologists, for which he received the cordial thanks of the president, Signor Capellini. He also prepared papers for the International Geological meetings which were held at Berlin and London. On June 4, 1885, he received an invitation to be present at the Berlin meeting of the International Geological Convention. In 1885 he began a sketch of the scientific work done in Indiana.

His days were never empty or dreary. When he was not competing among the celebrities of the old and the new world, he amused himself in lighter pursuits. He developed a technique for transferring photo prints to glass, or to chinaware, or he experimented with painting on wood or executing water colors on wood. He diversified his activity by reading technical journals as well as the popular ones; and upon noticing the formula for the construction of an Edison battery, on June 29, 1885, he developed one of his own. When friends, the Decker family, called upon the Owens on September 21, 1885, and informed Professor Owen that while they had attended the Vienna Exposition they had seen a cannon ball floating in a trough of mercury, he immediately floated a cast-iron bullet in a small vat of mercury. He shifted from physics to geology by abandoning specific gravity for the arrangement of fossils and he effected this transition as gracefully as a radio announcer glides from news items into advertising. After considerable experimentation he developed a technique for the drilling of glass with a common drill by keeping a solution of green camphor in equal amounts of alcohol and turpentine about the cutting edge of the drill. Having amused himself at that for a while, he read the accounts of the great lion tamer, Upelio Farmalie, who reported that the Cape lion was much more intelligent than the lion of Sahara. The Cape lion was almost untamable, even more difficult to tame than the leopard. The jaguar was very fierce. This was intellectual cantering after the race.

On his seventy-fifth birthday he called on many of his friends, and with each he left a calling card on which he had written, "The Seventy-fifth Birthday." Not being able to visit all his friends on one day, he extended his calling into the next. Each visitation yielded its harvest of good wishes, and the Grand Old Man of New Harmony began his seventy-sixth year feeling younger than when he closed the preceding one.

Cessation of teaching did not effect cancellation of correspondence with old friends in this country and abroad. With Professor Richard T. Ely, then at Johns Hopkins, he exchanged views on socialism; from Professor Campbell of Topeka, Kansas, he asked for information on tornadoes; and to Sir Richard Owen of England he confided his latest ideas on geology and physics. Entries in his diaries of letters written reveal an extensive mailing list which was in constant use.

Nor did he sever his relations with the lodges in which he held membership. He continued his regular attendance at the meetings of the Masonic Order and the Odd Fellows Lodge, and when the Omnipotent Potentate wanted an appropriate address for a special occasion, Professor Owen could always be counted upon to accommodate.

He lectured on a variety of subjects to Indiana and Illinois audiences. Within a wide radius he was in demand as a commencement speaker. He delivered the funeral oration over the remains of many residents, some of whom he knew intimately and many not too well. He called to congratulate young men when information reached him that they had won the hand of a young woman, and he extended his best wishes to the brides-to-be. He heard the wedding vows *gratis* of numerous young couples in Posey and the surrounding counties. He was host to Professor David Starr Jordan when he came to New Harmony to deliver a lecture. He introduced the distinguished educator to his fellow citizens. And although, because of deafness, he could not hear a word that was spoken, he displayed a vivid interest in the occasion, by mirroring in his own countenance the audience reaction.

Though he had been a regular attendant at the Presbyterian Church at Bloomington, in the absence of any church of that faith in New Harmony he worshipped in the Episcopal Church. At times he filled the pulpit of the Methodist Church in the morning and addressed the Epworth League in the evening. He met the Jewish Rabbi Sparger and heard him sing duets with various members of the Owen family.

Nor did he abandon his interest in medicine. In his scientific journals he read an "account of a singular disease in Peru and Bolivia." Among many professional volumes he read Breckinhoff's *Diseases of the Rectum,* and Popellon's treatise on hysteria. On October 2, 1882, he outlined notes for a paper on leprosy.

Without being a busybody he interested himself in the local school. There he lectured on his European travels and compared the systems of education of the various continental countries with the American. He suggested reading lists in geography and recommended dramatization of many historical events: "Let students enact such as *Ulysses, William Tell, Merchant of*

[97]

Venice, Marco Polo, Vasco de Gama and *William Wallace.*"
Professor Owen did not suggest how a village school could
secure properties needed for such comprehensive themes, but
had he been in charge of the projects he would have secured
them.

Though he was interested in public affairs, he never was
a candidate for public office. On October 17, 1885, he listed
the following topics as of significant interest: "(1) Temperance
problem, (2) Purifying of the Ballot Box, (3) Arbitration of
Capital and Labor, (4) Regulation of Immigration, (5) Recre-
ation, (6) Sunday Amusements, (7) States Rights Question
Again, (8) Mormonism, (9) Claiming that Persecution dictated
Edmonds Law, and (10) Civil Service." Four days after enum-
erating the above subjects, he was a dinner guest with James
G. Blaine at Evansville, Indiana. Though the Plumed Knight
had the reputation of being a dazzling platform personality,
Owen noted in his Diary, "I had a very pleasant conversation."

The Owen home in New Harmony was the center of gracious
and unostentatious hospitality. Formal dinner parties there
were rare, for he appreciated a treat to his intellect more than
he did a threat to his stomach. Friends and relatives called
in the tradition of the gay nineties and were welcomed without
fuss or excitement, but were made to feel that their presence
constituted a blossom on the Owen tree of time. Former colleagues from Bloomington came and spent several days; other
friends of former years, as well as relatives, came and went,
and between such visits Professor Owen sandwiched the reading
of a book or the writing of an article.

He continued his linguistic accomplishments during his last
few years. He translated French and German articles, read
Italian and Spanish essays; and on the occasion of David Starr
Jordan's visit to New Harmony he amazed his grandson, Richard
Dale Owen, by conversing with Jordan in Latin. In his Diary
for April 19, 1885, he notes that he had "read Greek."

He was eager to share his accomplishments with others, and so his home at times assumed the aspect of an extension center of Indiana University as he instructed anyone—usually youngsters—in any of his fields of learning. This included horsemanship and fencing, as well as dancing. As gracefully as his old joints would permit, he exhibited to his youthful spectators the various steps in the schottish, two-step, and waltz. He took groups into the fields and forests on nature expeditions, lecturing to them on botany, geology, and geography. Thus it is apparent that when he left teaching he retired to a strenuous life. For him life continued after seventy. He delighted in improving himself long after he left the classroom.

For some time before he quit teaching he had been burdened with delicate health. Soon after retiring to New Harmony he experienced a revival in energy which enabled him to enjoy his multifarious activities. This renewed vigor had fortified him for the long drives with horse and carriage to and from Bloomington; it had permitted him to attend the lodge and scientific meetings. But life expectancy for men after seventy is not encouraging, and the inevitable physical disability did not ignore him for long. He held indisposition at arm's length as long as he could by watchful consideration of his diet and sleep. Thus he omitted drinking chocolate during the summer months and did not resume it until September 16, in 1884. On January 5, 1885, he made the following entry in his Diary: "I am making dietetic experiment. I will record some and the conditions of health resultant, or supposed resultant therefrom:

> Temperature 26 degrees Fahrenheit, barometer high, wind S. E. Breakfast 1½ oz. bread & cup of coffee: 2 oz. of oatmeal and apple sauce mixed including water and a spoonful of cream, and one egg (2 oz.) total 10½ oz. Dinner: broiled chicken 2 oz. free from bone, one boiled potato weighing 5 oz., blue mange 3 oz., 3 oz. sago; total solid 13 oz.

Supper: Panada 2-3 oz. with some cream & sugar. Did not sleep well, perhaps on account of cream."

On the next day after he made the following entry in his Diary:

Breakfast: One slice of bread, 1 oz., 1 egg, 2 oz., oatmeal with cooking water, 3 oz., ½ cup of coffee. Total of 4 oz. of solids and 4 oz. of liquid.
Raining, but walked 1 hour.
Dinner: One slice of bread, 1 oz., 2 oz. of chicken (broiled) 3½ oz. of brownflour mush, 1 oz. of cream, 2 dates, ¼ oz.
Supper: One oz. of chocolate, 2 oz. of bread, 6 oz. of milk. After returning from theater drank milk and slept remarkably well.

Even though he catered to the whims of a delicate digestive system, he noted, "I am still taking a small quantity of the rye-wky, rock candy, glycerine and lemon in water after meals." But the best that a man with a degree in medicine and years of experience in teaching physiology could do was of little avail. He continued to complain of "feeling symptoms of chills," "too lame to take my exercises this morning," "chill, took quinine," "suffering from chills and fevers."

To the infirmity of deafness was added the difficulty of myopia. Yet he refused to wear glasses, for he maintained that the eyeball would alter its shape and improve his sight. Already his association with other people had become less agreeable because of difficulty in hearing their speech. To this was now added the reduced efficiency of his eyes. Professor Owen copied melancholy poetry into his Diary.

But he found more consolation in the close association with his family. He and Mrs. Owen took Thanksgiving dinner with one son and celebrated Christmas with the other. Now and then both sons with their families assembled at the paternal home, and in the presence of his children and grandchildren aches and pains, if not forgotten, were ignored.

Though considerably reduced in vigor and physical efficiency, he still continued his reading and looked forward with keen anticipation to attendance upon various scientific meetings during the summer of 1890. Periods of indisposition, however, recurred with greater frequency and longer duration. Consumption of mineral water, carried by a local grocery store, frequently had given him relief from physical distress, and on March 25, 1890, he meant to resort to the customary treatment. Unfortunately, a mortician in an adjoining part of the building which housed the grocery store had ordered embalming fluid on the grocer's stationery and the consignment had been sent to the grocer. The preservative had been stacked with the mineral water, and when Professor Owen and a local citizen asked for mineral water they were served, quite by mistake, the embalming fluid. Both took several swallows and both became violently ill. Professor Owen's friend recovered, but before the day was over Professor Owen had passed away. His remains are buried in the old cemetery in New Harmony under the epitaph of his choice: "His first desire was to be virtuous, his second to be wise."

BIBLIOGRAPHY

A. Unpublished Sources

Marie D. Fretageot's Letters, in the Library of the Workingmen's Institute, New Harmony, Indiana.

William Maclure Papers, in the Library of the Workingmen's Institute, New Harmony, Indiana.

Lazarus Noble, Adjutant General's Office, Letter and Order Book No. I, November 23, 1861-January, 1863 (Archives Division, Indiana State Library), Indianapolis, Indiana.

Richard Owen Papers, in possession of his granddaughter, Mrs. Aline Owen Neal, New Harmony, Indiana. These comprise letters, diaries, copies of speeches, and summaries of scientific experiments.

Richard Owen File, Archives Division, Indiana State Library, Indianapolis, Indiana.

Richard Owen Papers, Indiana University Library, Bloomington, Indiana.

Owen Papers, Purdue University Library, Lafayette, Indiana.

Julian Dale Owen Papers, in the Library of the Workingmen's Institute, New Harmony, Indiana.

Mathew R. Southard Papers, in Archives Division, Indiana State Library, Indianapolis, Indiana.

Josiah Warren Papers, in the possession of Mrs. E. Manlove, Indianapolis, Indiana. Photostats in Indiana State Library.

Posey County Circuit Court,
   Order Book F.
   Deeds, Records, vols. M, V.
   Marriage Records, vols. 1-2.
   Will Records, vol. B (1838-1852).

Minutes of Faculty Meetings of Indiana University, 1864-1879. Indiana University, Bloomington, Indiana.

Minutes of Executive Committee Meetings of Purdue University, 1872-1874, Lafayette, Indiana.

B. Published Sources

S. A. Cunningham Memorials: Col. Richard Owen, the Good Samaritan of Camp Morton . . . (Nashville, Tennessee., n. d.).

Hepburn, W. M., and Sears, L. M., Purdue University: Fifty Years of Progress (Indianapolis, Indiana, 1925).

Indiana House Journal, 1861, 1862.

Owen, Richard, (?) The Indiana School of Practical Sciences (n. d., n. p., New Harmony, Indiana, 1859).

Owen, Richard, *Report of Geological Reconnoissance of Indiana, Made During the Years 1859 and 1860* (Indianapolis, Indiana, 1862).

Pears, Thomas C., Jr. (ed.) *New Harmony, an Adventure in Happiness.*

Pears, Thomas C., Jr. (ed), *Papers of Thomas and Mary Pears (Indiana Historical Society Publications,* vol. 11, no. 1, Indianapolis, 1933).

Snedeker, Caroline Dale, "The Diaries of Donald MacDonald" *(Indiana Historical Society Publications,* vol. 14, no. 2, Indianapolis, Indiana, 1942).

The War of the Rebellion: A Compilation of the Official Records of the Union and Confederate Armies (8 vols. Washington, D. C., 1894-1895, 2 series).

C. *Magazines and Newspapers*

American Annals of Education and Instruction (Boston), n. s. (1841-43), (1850-51), (1851-52).

American Association for the Advancement of Science, *Proceedings,* 5 (1851).

American Geologist (Minneapolis), 1889.

American Journal of Education (Boston), n. s. 1 (1830).

"Treatment of Prisoners at Camp Morton," *Century Magazine,* XLII, 770 (September, 1890).

Indiana Magazine of History, (Bloomington), 12 (1916), 19 (1923), 36 (1940).

School and Society (Lancaster, Pa.), 57 (1943).

Blatchley, Willis S., "A Century of Geology in Indiana," *Indiana Academy of Science Proceedings,* 1916, pp. 89-177.

Browne, Charles A., "Some Relations of the New Harmony Movement to the History of Science in America," *Scientific Monthly,* 42 (1936): 483-97.

Estabrook, Arthur, "The Family History of Robert Owen," *Indiana Magazine of History,* 19 (1923): 63-101.

Fretageot, Nora C., "The Robert Dale Owen Home in New Harmony," *Indiana History Bulletin,* Extra Number, June, 1924, pp. 15-19.

Hartog, P. J., "Dr. Andrew Ure," *Dictionary of National Biography* (London), 57:335-36.

Jordan, David Starr, "Richard Owen," *Popular Science Monthly,* 51 (1897):259-65.

Brewster, Edwin T., "Course of Natural History at Hofwyl," *American Annals of Education,* n. s. 2 (1832):16-24.

E. Winchell, "A Sketch of Richard Owen," *American Geologist,* September, 1890.

Woodbridge, William C., "Sketches of Hofwyl," *American Journal of Education,* n. s. 1 (1831) 1-12.

Wyeth, John A., "Cold Cheer at Camp Morton," *Century Magazine,* LXI, 846, (April, 1891).

Bloomington *Post,* May 12, 1837.

Bibliography

Free Enquirer (New Harmony and New York), February 11, April 22, 1829, May 12, September 22, October 13, 1832.

Indianapolis *Indiana Democrat*, April 12, 1837.

New Harmony *Disseminator*, February 14, 21, 1835, n. s. 1:271, 280.

New Harmony *Indiana Statesman*, March 14, 1843.

New Harmony *Times*, December 16, 1838.

Indianapolis *Sentinel*, April 23, 1861, April 26, 1861, September 7, 1861, November 4, 1861, April 25, 1861.

Indianapolis *News*, May 8, 1914.

Indianapolis *Journal*, November 22, 1861, April 24, 1862, April 25, 1862, April 21, 1862.

LaFayette *Journal*, 1872-1874.

D. General Works

Hesseltine, William Best, *Civil War Prisons: A Study in War Psychology* (Ohio State University Press, Columbus, 1930).

Leopold, Richard W., *Robert Dale Owen. A Biography* (Cambridge, 1940).

Lockridge, Ross F., *The Old Fauntleroy Home* (New Harmony Memorial Commission, 1939).

Lockwood, George B., *The New Harmony Movement* (New York, 1905).

Podmore, Frank, *Robert Owen. A Biography* (2 vols., New York, 1907).

Schneck, J., and Owen, Richard, *The History of New Harmony, Indiana* (Evansville, 1890).

Snedeker, Caroline Dale, *The Town of the Fearless* (Garden City, N. Y., 1931).

Owen, Richard, *Key to the Geology of the Globe* (Nashville, 1857).

Owen, Robert, *The Life of Robert Owen by Himself*, with an Introduction by M. Beer (New York, 1920).

Winslow, Hattie Lou and Moore, Joseph R. H., "Camp Morton, 1861-1865, Indianapolis Prison Camp," *Indiana Historical Society Publications*, vol. XIII, No. 3. (An excellent piece of research of special value to the author in writing Chapter III.)

Printed in the United States
By Bookmasters